The ANC and the
Turn to Armed Struggle,
1950–1970

The ANC and the
Turn to Armed Struggle,
1950–1970

Ben Turok

First published by Jacana Media (Pty) Ltd in 2010
Second impression 2011
Third impression 2012

10 Orange Street
Sunnyside
Auckland Park 2092
South Africa
+2711 628 3200
www.jacana.co.za
Job No. 001730

ISBN 978-1-77009-968-5

Set in Ehrhardt 12/16pt
Printed by Ultra Litho (Pty) Limited, Johannesburg

See a complete list of Jacana titles at www.jacana.co.za

This book is dedicated to Moses Kotane, Michael Harmel, J.B. Marks, and those other leaders of the 1950s who were among the first to create a militant platform of struggle for national liberation inside and outside the country.
It is also a contribution to reflection on our history as the ANC celebrates a century of struggle and achievement.

Contents

FOREWORD

Comrade Ben Turok is a long serving member and leader of the liberation struggle. It is cadres like him who both in theoretical and practical terms helped shape the character and form of the struggle that was waged by the liberation movement against oppression in South Africa.

It was therefore not surprising that at a time when the battle against white supremacy had taken different forms of expression, operating underground and in conditions of exile that Comrade Turok was able to pen down the intricacies of what seemed very difficult to analyse.

"The Strategic Problems in South Africa's Liberation Struggle: A Critical Analysis" is one such tool that helped to search for theoretical weapons to deal with fundamental questions of our revolution. At a time when the question of unity amongst the forces for change posed a big challenge to maintain Comrade Turok's analytical work served to provide some of the answers.

It is therefore important to remember that all human struggles go through multiple phases and that each phase poses its own challenges. Comrade Ben was one of those gifted sons of the revolution who participated in the defiance of unjust laws campaign, the treason trail and the armed struggle before the banning of the liberation movement.

This work is of great significance today and that's the reason it cannot be underrated nor ignored. As we put our efforts in building the new South Africa and uniting all South African people for a common goal, the lessons learned in the fifties of the 20th century are not only important but relevant, if we want to avoid and not commit the same mistakes again.

In this work Comrade Ben Turok was able to piece together the threads of our revolutionary history and principles that were the theoretical foundation of the liberation movement and ultimately helped to inspire the march to the final victory over apartheid and racial division.

Students of history and political analysts will find the "Critical Analysis" worth reading.

KGALEMA MOTLANTHE

29 April 2010

Mpondo Revolt (photo courtesy of Mayibuye Centre, UWC)

Introduction

This book was written in Tanzania in 1968. It was a tough time for the movement: repression at home was at a peak, the external mission under OR Tambo often received a cool reception from many foreign governments, and the prospect of Umkhonto we Sizwe entering South Africa from its bases in Tanzania, Zambia and Angola was remote.

I was working for the Tanzanian government and only marginally involved in the military work of Umkhonto, although I was in constant touch with many top cadres. I therefore had time for reflection, study and writing, which resulted in this essay. The Liberation Support Movement of Canada published it under the title *Strategic Problems of South Africa's Liberation Struggle* and it received a great deal of attention throughout Western Europe and North America. Left groups of many orientations there were fascinated by the struggles of Third World liberation movements, not least those of Cuba, Mozambique, Angola and, of course, South Africa.

This text is published in its original form. This is because I believe that young cadres have not been adequately exposed to many of the ideological and policy debates of that time and what happened then, or understood the relevance of this period to our present environment. Many of these debates have still not been resolved. I hope that returning to this text will help to take us forward. It addressed the following issues.

Why the apartheid system was incapable of reforming itself

The essay briefly examines the conditions in which revolutions were launched in Vietnam, Mozambique, Angola and Guinea-Bissau, the forms of struggle, and the coalitions of forces that emerged. In South Africa there were no mediating institutions between the oppressor and the oppressed; hence sharp conflict was inescapable. It was therefore imperative to make an objective and concrete assessment of the balance of forces and their actual combination or potential and to launch political actions to realise that potential.

The necessity of a transfer of state power

The early decades of the ANC had a strong reformist tendency. At its formation, there were appeals to the government of the UK, followed later by calls for voting rights for people of colour, characterised as the extension of existing political rights to those excluded by the Act of Union. Even the call of the Defiance Campaign was for the abolition of six unjust laws and for a more fair social system.

Towards the end of the 1950s, as the apartheid system strengthened the discriminatory laws and its practices and became more repressive, it became apparent to the movement that not only was peaceful protest no longer tolerated, but that the system would never bend. Its overthrow was imperative. There was no other way.

In short, even though the early calls for racial equality were in a sense revolutionary, this does not mean that the ANC was constituted as a revolutionary movement.

The distinctive character of underground struggle

When the police disrupted campaign after popular campaign, and peaceful protest and organisation were met with state violence, it became necessary to create an underground apparatus. This process was accelerated during the 1960 State of Emergency when most of the top leadership and thousands of cadres were detained. Those who escaped the net immediately created an underground apparatus across the country. It operated with considerable efficiency because it was small and tightly disciplined from a security point of view.

With this change in operations came a new mindset: revolution was on the agenda. The creation of Umkhonto we Sizwe was the outcome. A new cadre corps emerged, deep under cover, isolated from normal social life and living as internal exiles. This change from open and legal protest politics did not come easily to many. Those who tended to drift back into the more comfortable style of the days of legal protest fell into the waiting jaws of the police state.

Only an underground apparatus could continue to operate – and it did so with some remarkable achievements, which are covered in the text.

The importance of African nationalist sentiment

Once revolution became the intention, it was clear that the goal was not merely the equal status and recognition of black people, but the transfer of state power to a liberation movement in which the African masses would play the main role. This meant articulating the consciousness of a distinct African identity within the context of a broader black coalition and its white democratic allies. The exclusively African membership of the ANC at the time was meant to give visibility to this approach.

The essay argues that it was well understood that 'the reinforcement of national consciousness lies deep within the [political and socio-economic] system'. Indeed, even workers saw themselves 'first as black and second as proletarians'. It argues further that 'non-racial democracy as a policy did not eliminate African identity', also recording that 'by the mid-1950s, African exclusiveness was condemned, charges of race-hatred denied, and [the structure and] platforms of the Congress movement reflected the active participation of all races'. Still, the importance of the primacy and visibility of African leadership was understood and accepted by all.

Attacks from the Pan Africanist Congress that these positions 'diluted the struggle' were rebuffed. The Freedom Charter consolidated the multi-racial dimension of our people and of the movement when it recognised once and for all that white people were intrinsic to the population as a whole.

The relationship of revolution and democracy

The early political aspirations of the ANC were expressed in the form of what the essay calls 'conventional democracy'. This model broadly accepted the institutional structures of the South African state, but demanded the extension of rights to the disenfranchised, as articulated in 'African Claims' in 1943. Access to parliament was the focal point of politics – although it was far from being the only arena. The ANC Youth League at the time adopted a different stance from African Claims, stressing the need for a resurgence of national consciousness to advance the struggle for national liberation.

The essay argues that revolutionary democracy goes beyond parliamentary elections. It is based on a notion of mass action aimed at the seizure of power by extra-parliamentary means, and the installation of a revolutionary government that would remove the previous incumbents and transform state institutions.

This position was based on the views of Marx and Lenin that no revolutionary movement could succeed without destroying the old state machinery and replacing it with new institutions and personnel.

In retrospect, the struggle over the 'sunset clauses' in the negotiations for democracy in 1993 took account of the experiences of revolutionary movements elsewhere.

The Communist Party and prospects for socialism

During the 1960s, the Communist Party established a presence in exile and gradually increased its influence within the top structures of the ANC and MK. Some of these comrades saw this as a way to influence the course of the struggle, but others may have been influenced by the history of the struggle in China and Vietnam where communist parties led the coalition of forces of the liberation movement.

There was also a debate within the movement about whether the South African revolution would first go through a democratic phase and then be followed by the socialist phase, as happened in Russia in 1917. The view that was largely accepted was that the South African revolution would make a transition, first democratic and then socialist, without significant ruptures along the way. A decisive break with the apartheid state form was necessary. And because of the progressive character of the leadership and cadres of the ANC, because of the existence of a class-conscious working class and trade union movement, because of the acceptance of the role and participation of the Communist Party, and because of the position of the ANC within the progressive anti-imperialist alliances in the international arena, this view assumed that an ANC-led liberation struggle would inevitably produce a progressive government.

Of critical importance was the view that there was no black bourgeois stratum to usurp power for their own interests – although a warning on this was inserted in the *Strategy and Tactics* document adopted at the 1969 Morogoro Conference: 'the national character of the struggle must … dominate our approach … Our nationalism must not be confused with chauvinism or narrow nationalism of a previous epoch. It must not be confused with the classical drive by an elitist group among the oppressed people to gain ascendancy so they can replace the oppressor in the exploitation of the mass.'

Thus, while the direct struggle for socialism was put aside in favour of a united front led by the ANC, with the installation of democracy as the immediate aim, no obstacles were put in place for the Communist Party to continue its advocacy of the ideology and theory of socialism.

This essay was written during a period of intense debate about the character of the liberation struggle, its objectives and methods of struggle. In our present concerns, as a ruling party focused on delivery, we have perhaps neglected the deeper concerns of the movement during the struggle years.

It is my hope that the republication of this essay will enrich our debates even now.

THE CONTEXT
Liberation Wars in the Third World

The sharp struggles in the 'Third World' in the last
decade have become internationally prominent for
more reasons than their drama. While progressives
everywhere have been stirred by the action of millions
of oppressed people, the political problems thrown up in
each case have also done much to stimulate interest and
commitment. The 'Third World' has become a most
important crucible of political experience. Sometimes
the equivalent of centuries of 'normal' development has
been compressed into a short time, bringing clearly into
the open the heart of politics, namely, who will hold
power and to what end. This function of crystallising
out the crucial questions of policy and strategy has
placed 'Third World' politics right at the centre of
international concern.

But a qualification is necessary. Although we
use the umbrella term 'Third World' to identify a
particular situation, we are not suggesting that there
is a single pattern of struggle. Rather, one is bound to

stress that in each case there is a unique combination of circumstances with peculiar strategies to match. We could hardly expect anything else in countries where class and national contradictions have not yet been clearly formed. Nevertheless, it is this variety of problems in the 'Third World' which makes it so challenging but which also makes it so obvious that there is no universal law of revolution.

Because the character of the social formations in 'Third World' countries is not yet fully formed, it becomes difficult for the outsider to identify progressive tendencies and to decide which movement is genuine and deserving of support. Too often sweeping generalisations based on a rigid theoretical framework have led well-meaning people to support the wrong group or to welcome what later turns out to be a retrograde tendency. There is no simple solution to this problem and I would argue only for a serious, historically concrete and specific analysis in each case to underpin our theory as the essential basis for determining where our support must go.

I want to suggest a number of factors that might help focus attention on what is important in determining the objective role of a movement. We have to identify, in the first place, which forces it represents and in what combination they occur. We need to try to assess the validity of the banner raised by the movement in its efforts to win mass support. Which political force is dominant in the movement is of great importance and we have to remember that in the relatively undeveloped socio-economic conditions of the 'Third World', textbook Leninist parties are not always available, nor can they always gain the leadership of the liberation forces. Finally, we have to evaluate the struggle methods proposed. In some cases the struggle takes on a revolutionary form with armed action the principal vehicle, while elsewhere political means are predominant. In yet other areas there is a combination of politically directed armed struggle together with various kinds of non-violent actions. This was the model in the early years of the Vietnam War.

Vietnam is also particularly instructive from the point of view of the political arrangements of the liberation forces. A broad coalition was established early on in which the most advanced socialist party combined with other parties to fight a People's War under the banner of national liberation from imperialism and for ending feudalism. The protracted nature of the war not only strengthened the coalition but it also confirmed the hegemony of the socialist forces.

In other areas the combination of forces has not been so felicitous and the direction the struggle takes is consequently erratic. In the Middle East, militant socialist Palestinians have been unable to set about their revolution in the way they would wish and have been caught up in a wider conflagration involving reactionary Arab states. The Palestinians are now dependent on these states, which are determining the parameters of the struggle. While the overall orientation of the war is progressive, the coalition of forces is constantly changing and the short-term outcome is yet uncertain.

In Africa, while everyone knows that the liberation wars of Frelimo, MPLA and PAIGC are making great inroads on Portuguese power; it is not equally well known that these movements are also deeply concerned with problems of political programme. There is an ongoing internal debate to ensure that progressive socialist tendencies are not relegated in the course of arousing a national response for People's War. Nevertheless, a separate socialist party is thought to be premature and too far ahead of the rump of the cadre force. Instead the revolution is being allowed to ripen in a way that will most favour the emergence of a social structure oriented towards socialism.

Each of these instances reveals a different combination of political forces arising, as they do, in differing circumstances. They nevertheless share in common the use of force. But in no case has armed struggle begun in a vacuum. There is always a threshold of 'normal' political struggle, and in the 'Third World' what is usually at issue is this: Under what conditions and at what stage does force necessarily enter the struggle equation? Chile has certainly destroyed any remaining illusions that force may be bypassed anywhere in the 'Third World', though it would not be easy to determine at what stage Allende might have saved his government by the use of force.

Whereas in the wake of Debray's famous polemic,

Revolution in the Revolution, many saw armed struggle as a single dimension of revolution, this is no longer the case. It is now recognised that there are many prior questions to be put, such as: When is the subjective strength of the movement sufficient for embarking on armed struggle? Do acts of terror and sabotage advance the struggle, especially in its initial stages? Do actions of this kind draw increasing support to the movement, or do they lead to isolation? Again, experience indicates that under certain conditions the very resort to force opens the way for a wide range of possibilities for mass participation, while in others it provides an excuse for the counter-revolution to clamp down on and liquidate the movement. So the question of how and when to start is critical, and the serious movement assesses its opportunities very carefully.

These questions are posed here because they are highly relevant to the situation in South Africa, which presents formidable problems for revolutionary theory. In South Africa, since there are no mediating political institutions between the authority of the ruling class and the mass of the oppressed, sharp conflict is inescapable. There is a huge disparity in lifestyles between oppressed and oppressors, and this in the context not of some archaic feudal state, but in the setting of a modern industrial society. It has been obvious for some time that there was no way out but revolution.

Yet the elaboration of a theory of revolution for South Africa has proved to be an extremely difficult task. This most complex of systems which combines the worst extremes of capitalism and colonialism in a matrix of harsh differentiation is remarkably resistant to ideal-type analysis. Looking back, it can be seen that this theoretical difficulty has inevitably spilled over into practical work where the strategic sweep and forms of struggle have yet to be elaborated successfully. Instead, there has been a great deal of sheer pragmatism, trying here, then there, to see where a chink in the white armour might reveal itself.

Among the theoretical questions that have been prominent is the problem of whether it is class or national liberation that is primarily at stake, and what the struggle consequences of such a determination might be. This issue has been central and the whole history of the movement has been marked by intermittent controversy between those who have pressed for an immediate socialist programme and for socialist hegemony, and those who have urged the more limited perspectives of national liberation as the first stage of the revolution. Within the latter position there has been a further spectrum ranging from the conventional democratic programme of the 'votes for all' variety and an alternative emphasis on exclusivist black nationalism.

To a certain extent practice came to the rescue. The question of programmatic perspective became clarified after Sharpeville and the State of Emergency when all hope of a non-violent solution collapsed. In the atmosphere of sharp confrontation between the rulers and the ruled it became necessary for the movement to specify who the enemy was that the new policy of sabotage and armed struggle was to attack. Was it the white government and its institutions? The white people as a whole? The 'system' of white domination (even here, its concrete form had to be established)? Or the capitalist system?

Once force was brought into the picture previous generalities about 'white superiority' and 'white *baasskap*' simply would not do. Once national liberation was understood to mean not just the achievement of equal status and recognition for blacks but the actual physical coming to power of the liberation movement, the movement had to be more clear about its own social base and the social forces it hoped to move into action.

This essay describes how some of these issues arose in the context of the South African liberation struggle over a period of some twenty years. In the course of the discussion some aspects of the struggle will have to be dealt with critically and it is hoped that readers will accept that this is not a matter of apportioning blame or making destructive criticism, but of improving our understanding of how particular methods came to be used and to what effect. This task is even more necessary since there are, even now, organisations inside the country which are repeating the errors of a decade ago.

Much of the material presented here was published

in two contributions to the *Socialist Register* of 1972 and 1973. I am particularly grateful to the LSM Information Centre for giving them an even wider airing and hope that this will not only facilitate a sharper determination of the goals and strategy of the South African liberation movement, but also that others in struggle may find some appropriate lessons in our experiences.

PART ONE
Non-violent Mass Action

In the South African liberation movement two tendencies have been in contest for supremacy for half a century. On the one hand, African (now black) chauvinism has made strident, and sometimes episodically successful, populist appeals to the black masses; on the other, the non-racialists have sought not only to uphold the goal of non-racial democracy, but also to mould the forms of the struggle in its image. The latter tendency has been the most persistent and is represented by the ANC and its allies.

This essay will argue that both tendencies have been pushed to unnecessary extremes as a result of inadequate specification of the goals and tasks of national liberation. It will urge that while non-racial goals are the only ones worth fighting for, and while only a non-racial perspective can open the way to a socialist society in the future, the main consideration of the liberation movement at present must be to reassess its policies in the light of the racial realities in South Africa today.

The principal feature of the peculiar social formation in South Africa is the sharp racial division which silhouettes the whites as beneficiaries extraordinary of the intense oppression and exploitation of the vast majority of black people. Consciousness of this condition is widespread among the masses, but the liberation movement has yet to find a way of articulating it adequately. A study of its publications over a long period shows that the movement has had the greatest difficulty in articulating formulations corresponding with the racial structure, which are capable of harnessing the 'national' sentiments of the most oppressed section of the population, the African people, and which nevertheless orient the revolution in a progressive direction.

Black Consciousness Is Not False Consciousness
Three explanations have been offered at various times of the nature of South African society. Some have attempted to define the system in the categories of class relations of mature capitalist society and they have produced a lifeless theory out of tune with reality. Others have tried to superimpose a purely colonial model, and this has led to a shallow explanation which does less than justice to the complexities of race and class. Most inadequate of all, however, are those of the liberal kind which assert that the South African brand of social injustice is entirely due to colour prejudice and the like. This is nonsense; apartheid is about a struggle for resources by coherent

18

interest groups. We can ignore the last explanation in the present discussion.

It has long been recognised that the presence of a large white minority made a very substantial difference to the prospects of overcoming colonial rule in Africa. This was seen to be the case in Algeria and in Kenya, and it remains true of the Portuguese colonies and Rhodesia. But what has not been reckoned with sufficiently is that in the South African case the white population is not only large (3,958,000), having entrenched itself over three centuries, but most importantly, it has established a modern industrial state. The process of transforming a colonial occupation (with a relatively large settler population) into a complex system based primarily on capitalist exploitation both direct and indirect has had enormous consequences for the African people. In a total population of 23 million, there are now 16,200,000 Africans, who are not only politically without rights, but who for the most part constitute a mass of property-less urban workers, farm labourers and semi-peasants. Despite separate tribal 'homelands', they are nevertheless conscious of a common destiny.

There are also 2,100,000 Coloured (mixed descent) people and 668,000 Indians, who, notwithstanding certain occupational, commercial and residential advantages compared with the Africans, are nevertheless equally without political rights and also subject to acute exploitation. The meagre political rights formerly held by these two groups have been whittled away to the point where illusions that they were somehow an in-between category with prospects of absorption into the arena of white power and privilege have faded away. This has been the result of the harsh application of colour bars even at the most petty level, reinforcing the separation between white and black. Unlike other capitalist ruling classes, South Africa's rulers have been forced by the inner logic of race domination to abandon policies of co-option and social bribery (the Bantustans excepted). Very little is done to legitimise its authority over any of the black national groups.

Thus, despite three centuries of cohabitation in one territory, social integration between black and white is non-existent, and consciousness of a separate black identity is general. Africans have always retained an awareness of a separate, historically constituted 'national' identity. Perhaps 'nationality' would be more accurate. At any rate, 'nation' here is not to be read as 'nation state'. Much African culture, especially language, remains, though it is true that modernisation has done much to break down tribal structures and bring new values and aspirations to many. But if integration into a modern industrial system has aroused desires for the fruits of that system, it has also brought a deep bitterness against the white people who deprive them of the unfettered use of even those products that have come their way.

The reinforcement of 'national' consciousness lies deep within the system. For the vast majority of blacks who are proletarians in town or country, their daily lives drive home the same lesson. And while a minority of blacks who, despite rigorous censorship, come to understand the processes of labour exploitation and the extraction of surplus value and develop a socialist consciousness, the structure around them confirms that they are first black and second proletarians. Whereas in a mature capitalist country uncomplicated by race divisions economic or trade union consciousness is generated spontaneously, in South Africa a sense of black deprivation is uppermost. Also reinforcing black awareness is the role and status of white workers. In no other country in the world is there so large a gap between those workers who perform skilled work and act in a comparatively supervisory capacity (white) and those who have lesser skills and mainly do the physical work, (African). Though there are a considerable number of African workers who do skilled work, it is not recognised as such.

The wage gap tells the story at a glance.

Industry White/African wage ratio
Mining 20.3/1
Manufacturing 5.7/1
Wholesale trade 5.1/1
Construction 6.6/1

Wages statistics, however, tell only part of the story. The gap between white and black (especially African) worker is marked by lack of trade union rights, low all–round status, minimal promotion prospects, sharp

21

differences in facilities at work and by the hundred-and-one other discriminatory practices of apartheid. Each of these exacerbates the cleavage between white and black at all levels, breaking the continuities and contacts that might be expected to develop at the work bench and leading to mutual hostility and polarisation on racial lines. Even the present tendency to absorb Africans into more skilled jobs that cannot be filled by whites due to skilled labour shortages has merely raised the colour bar floor-level. The white–black gap remains and the main effect of black upward job mobility is to give more supervisory jobs to whites. This in turn leads to higher wages, resulting in a further widening of the wages gap.

I do not stress the gap between white and black for the sake of exposing social injustice, nor in order merely to deplore racialism. That has been done often enough. I want instead to draw attention to the structural features of the system and in particular to show that black consciousness is not false consciousness as some dogmatic 'class only' theorists would have it.[1] Furthermore, it must be noted that an analysis in terms of race structures ought not to be confused with a discussion of race attitudes. The distinction is important since it helps us to grasp the point that conflict in this kind of racially structured system must necessarily work itself out along racial lines.[2] If this is not recognised because of a rigid adherence to class analysis or doctrine, the liberation struggle can only be impeded.

For instance, though it is clear that the white workers cannot be defined in any other terms than those of a top stratum of the working class, a class analysis omitting the political role of the white workers must mislead. It is not enough to say that the white workers constitute a labour aristocracy, that they have been bought off and that they are racist, though all this is true enough. What has to be stressed is that they have also been incorporated into the political and social realm of the ruling capitalist class and have a stake in the *status quo* in a way that ensures their loyalty, for at least the foreseeable future. It is a matter of structure, not of degree. It must be recognised that there is a deep and peculiar significance in the lot of black workers. Indeed, blacks are exploited and oppressed in a threefold manner – on the basis of race, as workers, and as a people.[3] In the South African case, therefore, the national question must be central both in our analysis and in the realm of praxis: this is the main point I wish to stress in the following discussion.

Many socialists fear that emphasising the national aspect of the struggle will somehow admit a black bourgeois solution or that the struggle will become so contaminated with racism that it will lose its sense of purpose and direction, leading only to a race war. It cannot be denied that these dangers exist and I shall try to deal with them later. Here we are looking at the formation of black consciousness, in particular among black workers.

Since most Africans and most blacks are proletarians, and since almost all employers are white, conflict over wages and general conditions of work, as well as overt political conflict, takes on a colour aspect. That the African proletariat, being the most exploited and oppressed of all, should play the most prominent role in this struggle ought to be clear from the preceding argument. But their role will be played out in national (race) rather than in class terms since this is how the contradictions manifest themselves.

But even outside the framework of industrial relations, black and white earnings and prospects, and therefore loyalties, are wholly different. Black petty traders, professionals, businessmen and civil servants are all clearly marked out by the stamp of colour, which acts with rigorous consistency in determining the place of people in the system. The polarity of race ensures that the difference of income and status within the black communities themselves tends to become diminished within a broader solidarity embracing a wider range of strata.

Just as a clear conception of common interest has grown among the whites who think only of defending their privileges,[4] so there emerges a counter-solidarity among blacks, and both tendencies seem to lessen the internal formation of class consciousness within the respective communities. For the black proletariat there can be no thought of liberation without an alliance of black people of the major strata. The abolition of the colour bar and of white privilege can only be achieved by an alliance of the black disenfranchised directed at the destruction of the white state apparatus. But recognition of this imperative grew only slowly in the South African liberation movement, and decades of appeals and protests had to work themselves out before the leap from reformism revolution could be made consciously, deliberately and publicly.

Early Concepts of Democracy

In the 1950s when the South African liberation movement, headed by the ANC, conducted a series of mass protest campaigns against white domination, the movement won large-scale support within the country. This vital struggle also gained considerable recognition internationally, and world sympathy and support for the black victims of apartheid was very great. Yet the campaigns of the 1950s failed to dislodge white power and few would argue that the methods of struggle of those days would be effective today.

This section sets out to investigate the political moments that led, in the first instance, to the use of non-violent mass action by the liberation movement, to assess their effectiveness and to trace the transfer to violence as a means to revolution. It concentrates on the political conditions that led to this form of confrontation between the white power structure and the extra-parliamentary opposition, and gives an account of the shifts in policy within the liberation movement as it changed its position in relation to the government and ultimately to the system as a whole.

It will be seen that the particular struggle methods used by the liberation movement at various stages in the 1950s were the product of particular choices made by the movement in response to new forms of repression. But there was an interaction between government and oppressed not only at the level of action, but also in the postures each took up in relation to the other. It is with this aspect, the outlook and perspectives that dominated the liberation movement, that we are concerned here since it is ultimately there that the explanation for changes in strategy and tactics can be found.

Fundamental transformation of society inevitably involves a fundamental change in the character of the governmental apparatus. In Russia the Soviets grew up as an alternative to the previous parliament; in China a wholly new governmental machine was created as Red Power established itself; in Cuba, Castro swept aside the whole rotten structure of the previous regime; and now in Chile it seems that Allende's defeat came primarily from his inability to change the character of the ruling assembly and the state apparatus.

There are, moreover, numerous instances, particularly in Africa and Asia, where the desire for fundamental change has been frustrated by the inability or unwillingness to develop new political institutions outside the old framework or to transform the existing ones meaningfully. The result is stagnation or retrogression. Those who seek to bring about fundamental change must examine critically the nature of the political structures they are challenging and be ready to reject them. Failure to do so may so hypnotise the movement as to tie it psychologically to a narrow sphere of policies and actions which take place within the framework of the old institutions. This issue is particularly important in the South African context where the political structure is undemocratic and the possibilities of constitutional political pressure by the mass of the people are blocked by rigid discriminatory barriers. The white minority imposes its rule on a disenfranchised and exploited black majority in a context of capitalist relations, and the horizontal stratification of power, privilege and wealth is overwhelming.

The system was not an invention of the present Nationalist government. It arose historically through the process of white colonisation which was carried out with the same devastating effects as elsewhere. However, in South Africa we find an additional dimension in that a white settler community established itself in the territory with every intention of remaining there permanently; and the indigenous black peoples were not incorporated in the evolving political superstructure. Although various minor openings were made for black participation, they were at no stage allowed to play an effective part in the system of government. Indeed, their efforts to exert communal pressure only led to greater repression.

Nevertheless, despite white exclusivism, the aspirations of the disenfranchised people have for half a century taken the form of a demand for a non-racial democratic system. But the form of the desired democracy has been expressed in different ways. On the one hand there has been what I shall call Conventional Democracy, which is based on a belief in the need to extend the existing parliamentary structure to embrace the black people. On the other hand there is a conception of Revolutionary Democracy, which envisages a seizure of power by the oppressed and the creation of a new state structure with a wholly new popular power-base which will give expression to the democratic will of the people as a whole and particularly its black majority.

The Conventional Democratic model accepted the structure of white power as a starting point but demanded the extension of rights to black national groups. Conventional Democracy saw parliament as the focal point for its demands though it also made resort to extra-parliamentary protests.

By contrast, Revolutionary Democracy focuses not on a white minority parliament but on the various existing discriminatory and oppressive institutions and sets its hopes on the generation of sufficient popular strength to set up an alternative and wholly different political structure. It hopes to seize power, probably by insurrection, as a result of direct confrontation with the white-manned state. In the ideology of the South African liberation movement there has been a transfer from the Conventional Democratic model to the Revolutionary Democratic model, and this has been accompanied by a transfer from non-violent to violent actions as a means of gaining political power. The roots of this transfer lay in the nature of the policies and decisions taken in the rough period 1945–52. This part of our discussion will be largely concerned with that period, since those were the crucial years determining the later transfer to violence; although the first violent actions were actually taken only in 1961.

ꙩꙩꙩ

The first elaboration of ANC policies in the modern period took place in 1945. Re-examination of the ANC's position was stimulated in part by the new mood which manifested itself after the war when the continent of Africa joined in the widespread demand by subject peoples for national independence and freedom. Furthermore, a significant change had taken place within South Africa itself in that the self-reliance forced on South Africa by the German threat to shipping boosted domestic industry, increasing the importance of African labour.

Since many skilled white workers joined the armed forces, Africans moved into semi-skilled jobs and the African labour force became more important both qualitatively and quantitatively.[5] In some industries Africans were allowed to join the registered unions even though they were legally barred from doing so, and the various organs of the labour conciliation machinery could be used to take up industrial complaints by Africans. A combination of these factors led to the growth of the urban African population, both in numbers and in its self-consciousness as a force to be reckoned with.

It was therefore natural that the ANC should seek to formulate new policies to accord with these developments. In 1943 a special committee of the ANC drew up a Bill of Rights, based on provisions of the Atlantic Charter, which came to be known as 'African Claims'. In the preface Dr A.B. Xuma, President General, said that they were pressing 'our undisputed claim to full citizenship' and that 'a just and permanent peace will be possible only if the claims of all classes, colours and races for sharing and for full participation in the educational, political and economic activities are granted and recognized'.[6] Dr Xuma distinguished between two classes of self–determination. 'In certain parts of Africa it should be possible to accord Africans sovereign rights and to establish administrations of their own choosing. But in other parts of Africa where there are the peculiar circumstances of a politically entrenched European minority ruling a majority non-European population the demands of the African for full citizenship rights and direct participation in all the councils of the state should be recognized. This is most urgent in the Union of South Africa.'

Recognition by the ANC of the existence of a

permanent white community in South Africa, making it a special case, needs to be underlined. This acceptance greatly influenced the nature of the demands made by the ANC. In the section called 'Bill of Rights,' the document calls for the 'extension' to all adults of the democratic freedoms set out in the Atlantic Charter and was formulated in terms of what I have called Conventional Democracy.[7] But it is important to note that the Atlantic Charter freedoms were modified to suit South African conditions, and particular stress was given to the abolition of all acts of discrimination on grounds of race and colour. There was much emphasis on the abolition of segregation, which 'is designed to keep the African in a state of perpetual tutelage and militates against his normal development'.

The men who drew up African Claims were mostly professionals, clerics and lecturers, Africans who had somehow risen above the mass and were then the natural leaders of a nationalist movement. They were mostly men of moderation described two years earlier by E.T. Mofutsanyana, Secretary for Labour in the ANC Executive: 'It will be seen that from its inception, Congress thus was wedded to a timid and reformist conception of the status of the African people. Lacking any clearly formulated long-term policy, Congress limited itself to immediate partial struggles against one or other aspect of discrimination. But it did so with vigour and militancy.'[8] African Claims was meant to bring greater coherence into ANC policy and it did indeed establish the basic principles that were to guide policy for a long time.

On the face of it, these principles could be read as bourgeois democratic demands and they have been interpreted by many writers on South African history in this way. For instance, the first full-scale history of the ANC says this of its policy: 'Freedom involved neither national independence nor a socialist revolution, but freedom for individual achievement and a non–European contribution to the wider society ... At its core this involved a belief in non–racialist principles and envisaged a future South African society characterised and enriched by the growing interdependence and cooperation of its various population groups within one economic and political order.'[9]

This interpretation is a little naive. African demands for the right to enter freely into the economic system could not, in the context of South African conditions, be described in these terms. Since the colour bar was, and is, functional in maintaining white privilege and wealth, the demand for its abolition was necessarily far–reaching. Yet it is also true to say that the full implications of these demands were not worked out. Sampson is probably right when he says that the ANC adopted what was in effect a minimum programme which satisfied the aspirations of all sections of its membership, leaving it open to differing interpretations.[10]

My point is that these demands, however radical in their long-term implications, were nevertheless articulated as 'extensions' of the freedoms enjoyed by whites. In this limited sense, I call them Conventional Democratic demands.

A Militant 'Programme of Action'

At the very time that African Claims was under discussion, a group of young nationalist-minded intellectuals was being formed within the ANC. They were led by Lembede, Mda, Tambo, Sisulu and Mandela (the last three later becoming leaders of the ANC). Lembede propounded a policy of fighting for African independence, freedom from domination by other national groups and the establishment of an African nation. An important dimension to their outlook was the insistence that the mother body should cease merely making representations to a stubborn white government and engage in more serious action. As Sampson put it: 'For thousands of politically- minded Africans 1946 was the year in which they ceased to have serious hopes of a change of heart among Whites, the year in which the Youth League won its point over the Old Guard of Congress.'[11]

The policy of the ANCYL was that acceptance of the white minority in South Africa was conditional. 'But we insist that a condition for inter-racial peace and progress is the abandonment of white domination and that the basic structure of South African society should be such that those relations that breed exploitation and human misery disappear.'[12] Walshe

33

says: 'Whereas African Claims had set out the aspirations of congressmen in terms of the non-racial and inherent right of individuals, the policy statements of the CYL went one step further. They accepted the goal of eradicating racial discrimination as the means to untrammelled African progress, but went on to declare the African political intention and urgent need as being the assertion of his numerical majority. This was to be used for restructuring society at the dictates of African nationalism intent on the exercise of power, even if it was prepared to tolerate permanent racial minorities.'[13]

The ANC was considered too tame by the Youth Leaguers. They rejected the notion expressed in the ANC constitution of 1943 of the need 'to educate parliament ... [And] other bodies and the general public regarding the requirements and aspirations of the Native people' and 'enlist the support' of sympathetic 'European societies, leagues or unions' who might be 'willing to espouse the cause of right and fair treatment of Coloured races'.[14]

The Youth League argued that this was the language of supplication and devaluation of the national image of African people. They wanted to give prominence to African nationalism as a specific ideology and urged that it be used to build up the organised strength of the mass of Africans as the base from which to press for political rights.

The constitution of the ANCYL declared as its aims (a) 'To arouse and encourage national consciousness and unity among African youth', and (b) 'To assist, support and reinforce the African National Congress, in its struggle for the National Liberation of the African people.'[15] No mention was made of the 'united democratic South Africa', which was one of the main points in the 1944 constitution of the mother body.[16]

However, the Youth Leaguers had some way to go before they could consolidate their position. They operated as a faction within the ANC and had the full weight of conservatism of that body to overcome. Most of them were students or recent graduates and their activities were limited by the absence of a mass base in the main cities.

The situation changed, however, when the National Party came to power in 1948. In the midst of the tensions surrounding this unexpected event, the Youth Leaguers emerged as leaders within the ANC National Executive, though they were working under the leadership of Dr Moroka, President General, who was a well-known professional man and not a militant. But this has been the ANC style. A man of exceptional public standing has taken the helm of the organisation so that it is seen to speak in the name of the broadest sweep of African opinion as a national movement. At the same time, militants have been able to take a prominent place on the executive committee and press the pace.

The change of leadership was coincident with an alteration in policy. In 1949 the famous Programme of Action was adopted which set out the demand for national freedom: 'Freedom from White domination and the attainment of political independence. This implies the rejection of the conception of segregation, Apartheid, trusteeship or White leadership which are all in one way or another motivated by the idea of White domination or domination of the Whites over the Blacks. Like all other people the African people claim their right of self-determination.'[17]

The phrase 'attainment of political independence' was ambivalent in that it expressed a desire for freedom but still within the single South African body politic. (It demanded 'the right of direct representation in all the governing bodies of the country'.) A possible explanation is that the purpose of the phrase was to give expression to the growing recognition that whites would not simply hand over power to the black majority and that Africans would have to exercise some form of *coercion* to get their way. At the same time there was little clarity about the way coercion could be brought to bear and this problem was not worked out clearly for another decade. Furthermore, how there could be a transfer of power to enable Africans to attain their freedom was to bedevil ANC policy in its future campaigns. African nationalism, even the African Revolution, did not come to mean the seizure of power or the overthrow of white authority. Its militant formulation was still within the framework of Conventional Democracy.

This can be seen from the terms of the Programme itself. Para 3 states: 'Appointment of a council of action whose function should be to carry into effect, vigorously and with the utmost determination, the programme of action. It should be competent for the council of action to implement our resolve to work for: (a) the abolition of all differential political institutions the boycotting of which we accept and to undertake a campaign to educate our people in this issue and, in addition, to employ the following weapons: immediate and active boycott, strike, civil disobedience, non-cooperation and such other means as may bring about the accomplishment and realisation of our aspirations. (b) Preparations and making plans for a national stoppage of work for one day as a mark of protest against the reactionary policy of the Government.'[18]

The document therefore raised sharply the need for militant mass action even to the point of civil disobedience and a political general strike. It also broke new ground in calling for non-collaboration on a mass scale. But, even though it raised the issue of the attainment of political rights and therefore political power by Africans, it did not pose the idea of revolution. Throughout the succeeding decade, even when mass action and political consciousness and commitment were at their height, the conditions within which a transfer of power from a white minority regime could be effected were not articulated.[19]

The explanation for this is difficult to pin down, though this weakness came to hamper the development of actions proposed in the Programme of Action. Part of the explanation must lie in the character of leadership of the ANC, which had not yet shed its moderates. In part it was also due to the inhibiting effect of prohibitions in the Suppression of Communism Act of 1950, which defined communism widely as the advocacy of 'social and political change'. But there were other factors too, which will emerge later in this essay.

The immediate purpose of the proposed militant mass action was clear enough. It was meant to:

a Generate a spirit of resistance to oppression;

b Develop political consciousness;

c Create new organisational structures;

d Bring into sharp focus discriminatory laws and harsh measures, i.e. expose how the colour bar worked in practice; and

e Bring the oppression in South Africa to the attention of the world.

Bold as the Programme of Action was, it was not immediately brought into effect. The struggle within the ANC for a more militant line had taken a great deal of its energy, and factional activity reduced the effectiveness of the organisation nationally. Some observers considered that the organisation was tearing itself apart over leadership claims while the mass work envisaged by the Youth League in the mid-1940s was not being attended to sufficiently. Yet the pressures were building up as the Nationalist government set out to fulfil its election promises of tackling the 'agitators' and implementing its policy of apartheid. When the time for action came, the

ANC was to find itself in harness with the Communist Party, which had been pressing forward on its own account, but whose path converged increasingly with that of the ANC as government repression mounted.

The South African Communist Party had been extremely influential in the militant struggles of the opposition forces since its foundation in 1921. Founded by militant, mainly white socialists, many of whom were active in the white trade union movement, it switched its focus to African liberation in the 1930s when it adopted the Black Republic slogan. While this policy corrected an excessive preoccupation with white trade union politics and brought up sharply the question of African liberation, the policy was brought into effect in a high-handed manner which led to tremendous internal struggle. Just when the party was recovering its equilibrium, it was thrown off course once more by the Second World War.

Many senior white communists joined the army to fight against fascism and the party as a whole gave much attention to the worldwide anti-fascist struggle. After the war, when the party might have once more turned its main attention to the problems of African liberation and the class struggle, the emergence of a strong fascist movement under the umbrella of Afrikaner nationalism constituted a fresh challenge at home. Two contradictory strands emerged in CP policy. One sought to give the main thrust of its energy to the struggle of the black people, and the other gave primacy to the mobilisation of a broad united front against the Afrikaner fascist threat.

The ambivalence of the CP's position is best shown in the resolutions adopted at a Special Conference in 1949. In the section headed 'Race Oppression and the Class Struggle' it stated: 'The outstanding feature of the Nationalist Party is not its racialism and its class character but its marked leanings towards a dictatorship of a Fascist kind.' Yet, under the heading 'Non-European Resistance Movement' we find: 'The reactionary, fascist character of the Nationalist Government is to be recognized, in the first place, in its attitude to the Non-European people.'[20]

This resolution, like much of the earlier comment in the CP paper, *The Guardian*, shows why its activities on the anti-fascist front led it to be drawn either into seemingly defending existing parliamentary institutions against National Party attacks, or into creating illusions about the possibility of 'extending' the degree of existing democracy to the black people.

It seems that the Party was importing the idea of the United Front from Europe, where it had been used to rally opposition to the fascist forces among a people which was homogeneous in a parliamentary sense, to a wholly different situation in South Africa. In South Africa there could not possibly have emerged a United Front of white anti-Nationalists in alliance with the black people. The movement failed to draw the line of demarcation in the correct place, and this failure led to seeking alliances which were illusory.

At the same time it is evident that the tendency to give excessive attention to the parliamentary scene was not limited to the CP alone. It continued throughout the 1950s and white parliamentary rivalries continued to absorb the whole movement and feed illusions about peaceful change for a considerable time.

But the CP was by no means wholly involved in parliamentary and constitutional policies. Some of its best cadres and leaders were in fact extremely active in the extra-parliamentary mass movement usually in close association with grassroots ANC branches, and the history of the late 1940s is filled with the story of events of considerable moment. These can be dealt with only very sketchily here.

CP activists, for example, were deeply involved in trade union work and this led to significant all-round growth and militancy. There were 304 strikes officially recorded during 1939–45 with Africans participating in many of them. In 1944 thousands of African squatters occupied vacant land around Johannesburg, refusing to move until the City Council built houses for them. Their battles with the authorities and police became legendary, and the black belt to the west of Johannesburg continued to be the best recruiting ground for the political movement for a long time. In 1944–5 there was a widespread ANC–CP anti-pass campaign which did much to arouse mass feelings on this the most oppressive of South Africa's race laws. In June 1946, the

Smuts government passed an anti–Indian measure (the Ghetto Act) which brought 2,000 Indian volunteers into action in breach of the law. The campaign was led by the South African Indian Congress.

In 1946 the African miners' union called a strike which was supported by 70,000 workers despite intense repression in the mining compounds where they were forced to live. Armed police attacked the strikers, opened fire and charged them with bayonets. After the strike the leaders of the union were arrested, together with a number of leading CP members, and charged first with bringing Africans out on an illegal strike and then with sedition.

With the election of the National Party in 1948 a new list of repressive measures was placed on the statute books and political tension rose throughout the country.

Some local struggles were fought over train apartheid in Cape Town, a bus boycott was carried out in Moroka Township, Johannesburg, and police raids for passes led to clashes between Africans and police at Newclare, Johannesburg. On 16 February 1950 *The Guardian* reported: 'Five times in the last six months bloody clashes between Africans and police have taken place on the Rand. Many Africans have lost their lives and many police have been injured in these clashes which have at times developed into running gun fights in which whole communities [including white civilians] have been involved.'

In all these events communists played a significant

part and as a result of intense activity at grassroots level the Party established close links with rank-and-file members of the trade unions and the ANC. Even when relations were somewhat strained between the CP and the ANC leadership, the CP was still influential at the lower levels.

Political currents were now flowing swiftly and all the parties and movements were being caught up in the tensions gripping the country. The government was pressing on with its measures to ban the Communist Party and a national conference of the Party called for a positive campaign both 'inside and outside parliament'.[21]

The conference resolution struck an exceptionally clear note. 'Recognizing the struggle for national liberation of the oppressed peoples of SA is bound up with the struggle for socialism, the CP will continue as it has done in the past to resist all forms of racial and national oppression. The national liberation organisations of the Non-European people of SA as well as the CP and the whole working class have a vital part to play in the struggle for equality and justice. We pledge ourselves to support them and join them in this struggle.'[22]

In taking this stand on the question of national liberation and by encouraging its cadres to work among the mass of the people on local issues, the CP was laying the basis for an alliance with the ANC, which it had previously regarded as a reformist, petty-bourgeois-led movement more given to internal wrangling than fighting the enemy In fact, events were pushing both organisations towards unity and towards confronting the oppressive state, though in retrospect it is remarkable how long it took to cement this alliance in practice.

At the level of policy the crucial determinant of combined militant mass action was the adoption by the ANC of the Programme of Action. This 1949 Programme of Action transformed the ANC from a cautious body into a dynamic mass movement.[23] It urged non-collaboration and refusal to cooperate in oppressive measures. But non-collaboration was not thought of negatively, as mere withdrawal, it was a positive attitude involving coercion of the government.[24] The 1949 ANC conference linked 'uncompromising non-collaboration' with boycotting all bodies set up by the government to represent Africans and decided to stage a one-day general strike at some date to be set.[25] The government certainly interpreted this policy as coercive in intention and raised the alarm among the white population.

The CP was at first dubious about the concept of 'non-collaboration'. It had used its odd 'African Representatives' in parliament and the Cape Provincial Council as effective propagandists, and many African Advisory Boards and Residential Associations in townships had been useful in mobilising the masses. Furthermore, Communists had spent a lifetime working in trade unions and they were fully conversant with the use of limited institutions for organising purposes. In addition, the CP had for long been engaged in a battle with the sterile Unity Movement in the Cape, which engaged in furious polemics about the principle of boycott and 'non-collaboration' but avoided political action. The CP had argued that boycott was a tactic and not a principle and was only to be used where it led to specific gains.

A conference resolution of early 1950 stated their position: 'Conference notes that the ANC and AAC [All African Convention] have decided to use the weapon of "non-collaboration". If this means nothing more than the resignation of individuals from public bodies it will in fact be a retreat and a screen for inactivity. It will play into the hands of the Government. Like all other political tactics "non-collaboration" is a weapon to be used at appropriate times and in favourable circumstances. Backed by organized mass action "non-collaboration" as a weapon will be the means of arousing the people to a more intensive and higher form of struggle. But the emphasis must be placed at all times on mass struggle.'[26]

Despite continuing disagreements between the ANC and CP, the ANC President General, Dr Moroka, acting in his individual capacity, met with leaders of the Indian Congress and CP to sink their differences and unite against the government by calling for mass protests on May Day and 26 June (Freedom Day) in 1950. In the May Day protest 18 Africans were killed by police fire at Newclare, Johannesburg.

As a reaction to this brutality, a Joint Planning Council was set up consisting of three Africans and two Indians; it included Dr Moroka and Dr Dadoo (who was a leader of the Indian Congress and a leading member of the CP). The protests mounted and there were a number of clashes between protesters and police involving a loss of lives. Police brutality was strongly condemned by the Council while at the same time they also dissociated themselves from violence as a political means.

The 26 June 1950 strike was called a 'unique demonstration of unity' by the National Day of Protest Coordinating Committee, which said it was a 'first step towards our liberation'. Dr Moroka thanked the supporters of the action and said: 'The step we took was taken after all other possible avenues of coming to some understanding with the SA Government had been fruitlessly explored. It is the only language we think the Government can understand. Our respect for law and order is not something we put on for occasions. It is part and parcel of our nature. But there can be no lawlessness where the laws are such that they cannot be obeyed.'[27]

It was in these terms that Dr Moroka presaged the defiance of unjust laws which was to bring the liberation movement into direct conflict with the state machine throughout the country.

The Defiance Campaign
The Nationalist government, now well established in office, set about exploiting to the full its election cry

of '*swart gevaar*' (Black Peril) and 'communist menace'. Having promised the electorate that it would take strong action against all forms of 'subversion', it passed the Suppression of Communism Act, which made it possible to outlaw the Communist Party. The CP accordingly dissolved itself by decision of the Central Committee, though it later criticised itself severely for not taking the organisation underground. It was lost sight of for ten years though it actually regrouped secretly from about 1953.

The implications of the Suppression of Communism Act were not lost on the ANC. They knew that the Communist Party was merely the first victim in a process of proscription of public organisations (it was itself banned in 1960) and that the Act could be used to ban individuals who were not communists. The government was in fact bringing into a common stream some of the various extra-parliamentary opposition movements by virtue of its oppressive measures.

For its part, *The Guardian*, now the only public spokesman for the remnants of the Communist Party, gave greater stress to 'non-Europeans' as the centre of gravity of the forces of change. It said on 12 July 1951: 'The only force capable of bringing about a radical change in the SA political scene is the Non-Europeans … The time has come for a SA chartist movement. For too long has the white man ruled without consideration for the needs of the black man. But if the white man has been callous, it is equally true that he has been aided in his self-indulgence by the inability of the Non-European people to speak with a voice of power.'

The emphasis on non-Europeans and the demand for the vote were bound to appeal to those elements in ANC who had previously been hesitant about an alliance with the CP. The views of the rising new leadership within ANC were summed up by Nelson Mandela at the December 1951 ANC Conference. 'Addressing the conference on methods of political struggle, Mr N. Mandela opposed the conception of a Non-European front with the immediate aim of halting the growth of fascism. Fascism was being smuggled in by a back door behind a screen of fear of supposed black risings and of "Communism". The conditions favouring fascism could not be removed so long as the African was kept in subjection. The Africans, because of the numbers, should be the spearhead of an organized political struggle to demand full democratic rights ... Apartheid had to be disorganized and made unworkable.'[28]

Close cooperation within the liberation movement was given further impetus at a meeting convened by ANC in August 1951 of the joint executives of the ANC, Indian Congress and Franchise Action Council (a Cape, largely Coloured, organisation). The CP had already been dissolved, but important communists were there. The meeting established a Joint Planning Council which was to plan and set in motion a mass campaign against six oppressive laws: the Pass Laws, stock limitation, the Group Areas Act, the Separate

Representation of Voters Act, the Suppression of Communism Act and the Bantu Authorities Act.

The most significant aspect of the plan evolved by this Joint Planning Council was that although it was based on 'non-cooperation' it was in fact defiance of unjust laws that was intended. And though the focus was on six laws, the hope was, as Mandela's speech indicated, that the campaign would develop a mass character which would somehow 'disorganise' the government. Highly significant too, was the first date chosen for the commencement of what became the Defiance Campaign. It was the 6th of April, the tercentenary of Jan van Riebeeck's arrival at the Cape. It marked 'the advent of European settlers in the country, followed by colonial and imperialist exploitation which has degraded, humiliated and kept in bondage the vast masses of the non–white people'.[29]

The Plan of Action proposed the defiance of unjust laws in three stages:

1 Selected personnel to go into action in various centres.
2 The number of volunteer corps to be increased as well as the number of centres of operation;
3 The stage of mass action where the countrywide struggle assumes a general mass character involving both urban and rural people.

Industrial action was considered to be the 'best and most important weapon' but it was too early to be used at that stage.

The setting of the scene for the Defiance Campaign is of considerable importance since it shows the political perspectives of the liberation leadership. But it must be remembered that they were working within the shadow of the Suppression of Communism Act, which prohibited the advocacy of social, political and economic change. There were other wide-ranging laws which limited what could be said publicly. Nevertheless, the vast quantity of material available on this period, and the persistence of certain elements of policy, make judgements on some aspects possible. Even if there were other private policies and thoughts, one could argue that these were not put out for general consumption and they cannot therefore have been influential in determining the course of events. In the end, we are left with the material which is to hand but with the reservation on caution mentioned above.

Many observers have noted the controlled language in which the Defiance Campaign was put to the people. Great stress was given to the non-violent aspect of the proposed action. Attention has also been drawn to the fact that the liberation movement went through an elaborate ritual of writing to the Prime Minister warning him of their intentions and demanding the 'restitution' of democratic liberties to the oppressed people. In his speech at the ANC Conference in December 1951, Dr Moroka said: 'We are South Africans and we ask for the political status of South Africans. Yet we are regarded as enemies. From the government of South Africa we ask for nothing that is revolutionary.'[30] But the government did not see the matter in this light. In his reply the Secretary to the Prime Minister said: 'This is not a genuine offer of cooperation, but an attempt to embark on the first steps towards supplanting European rule in the course of time.'[31]

We see then that at the start of the campaign the ANC was proposing a controlled operation of defiance of certain laws in order to abolish those laws in a context of the achievement of African freedom. It was put forward as a mass campaign, even open-ended in its perspectives as in stage 3, but nevertheless non-violent and orderly, with a clear invitation to the government to meet the demands of the people in a reasonable manner. The note of grievance was combined with an air of legitimacy.

Yet some of the speeches and statements were contradictory. *The Guardian*, a major paper of the liberation movement at this stage, continued to give much space to the parliamentary battle over the representation of the Coloured people. It expressed great anxiety for the 'defence of the law'. The same paper spoke about the danger of a *coup d'état* by means of forcing through the 'High Court of Parliament Bill' (*The Guardian*, 8.5.1952) and Kotane, Secretary of the former CP, wrote: 'unless the combined opposition of the people is able now to defeat the first steps to dictatorship the government, fearing the outcome of a straight election, will use its sweeping powers to frustrate the people's will.'

Some of the statements of the day indicate that even while the liberation movement was being geared to serious mass struggle, its leaders were to some extent hypnotised by constitutionalism and legalism.[32] Perhaps the masses had not as yet responded as vigorously as expected to the spate of repressive measures brought in by the new government, and in the absence of mass militancy the leaders were carrying on the political battle at the same level as before. Perhaps they were themselves unable to adapt to the new semi-legal conditions. Perhaps it was due to the still considerable protection afforded by the courts, which had not yet been infiltrated by Nationalist appointees and which still maintained a semblance of legal integrity, though the law itself was of course an instrument of colour bar rule and repression even then.

The liberation movement did indeed score considerable successes in the courts. Not only were many individual prosecutions defeated by skilled legal argument but even major legislative battles were won by resort to the courts. For instance, apartheid on trains was defeated by a court ruling that facilities which were separate must also be equal. All these victories led to illusions that government inroads on popular rights could be rebuffed by legal action. Nevertheless, despite the extensive courtroom sparring, the long-awaited Defiance Campaign began and rapidly gained momentum.

The Defiance Campaign was a major landmark in the history of the liberation movement. Batches of resisters went into action by deliberately breaking racial prohibitions on certain facilities. Volunteers openly and deliberately broke rules on where black and white could sit, travel or queue. They infringed movement restrictions, squatted in places reserved for white occupation and transgressed many of the numerous rules that constitute the system of race segregation. Many leaders broke their banning orders. They were arrested and other 'defiers', as they were called, followed on. The campaign spread to all the cities and many small towns throughout the country. Over 8,000 activists were arrested for 'defying', while a vast number of people took part in the meetings and protests which accompanied it. Political activity was at a peak throughout the five months of its duration.

The end of the campaign coincided with a government proclamation prohibiting incitement of Africans to resist and contravene any law and banning meetings. This proclamation was subsequently reinforced by the Public Safety Act and Criminal Amendment Act which imposed very severe penalties for incitement to break the law by way of protest.

But some commentators have argued that it was the violence that broke out in October and November, five months after the commencement of the campaign, which brought it to a halt. Individual acts of violence that set off riots occurred at Port Elizabeth on 18 October,

Denver, Johannesburg, on 3 November, Kimberley on 8 November, East London on 11 November, and Langa (arson) in December. Kuper, who made the most thorough study of the Defiance Campaign, has said: 'Though the immediate causes of the riots are obscure, their effects were to damp down the spirit of resistance. It is, of course, conceivable that the campaign had reached its peak prior to the rioting and was, in any event, in process of decline.'[33]

A welter of explanations has been offered on the significance of the Defiance Campaign, and it is considered to be an important model of non-violent mass action with considerable relevance to other situations. But much confusion remains on this campaign. For instance, Kuper said in 1953:

'No immediate claim is made for direct political representation and for full democratic rights, which are held out as a goal for the future. The time element is thus conceived in the spirit of Liberalism. It is evolutionary, but with a perspective within the span of perception – "within our lifetime" – as the leaders of the resistance movement phrase it.'[34]

Much later, however, in 1970 Kuper revised his analysis: 'What the Congresses in fact planned was not simply a civil disobedience campaign but a social, economic and political revolution by graded steps ... The graded steps by no means implied a process of evolutionary change. On the contrary, the abolition of unjust laws was merely a sort of trailer for the main piece, a revolution to achieve racial equality; and this revolutionary goal was made quite explicit in the notices of intention communicated by the Congresses to the Government. But even if the Congresses had announced only quite modest reforms, their goal would still have been a revolution for racial equality.'[35]

This remarkable change in perspective is symptomatic of the difficulties the Defiance Campaign has presented for those who want to interpret it strategically in a historical context. The problem might be of purely academic interest except that in 1960 the ANC was once again setting out on a Defiance Campaign, this time with 'no defence', 'no fines' and 'no bail'. (It was pre-empted by the PAC, who got wind of the plan.) In 1972 members of the Coloured Labour Party once again broached a campaign of non-violent resistance and it is not unlikely that a similar campaign may develop in the near future. The point is that where laws and practices are overtly discriminatory and where some scope for open organisation exists, non-violent mass resistance campaigns are bound to arise.

The first aim of the Defiance Campaign was to bring into the sharpest focus the oppressive character of the discriminatory laws in South Africa. Such acts as sitting on post office benches reserved for whites were meant to bring race discrimination out in the sharpest form, while the breach of other regulations was intended to show up the oppressive nature of these laws. The technique was used as a propaganda weapon to highlight for the country as a whole, and not least for the non-whites themselves, that the system of discrimination was unjust and oppressive.

The Congresses sought to maintain a posture of legitimacy throughout the campaign and gained widespread support from previously uncommitted black South Africans. The campaign also helped jolt the conscience of white democrats and liberals,[36] though it failed to move the bulk of whites. Instead, as the campaign progressed, white opposition and unity hardened against the resisters.[37]

The second aim of the campaign was to bring pressure to bear on the government by way of open resistance to official policy, even though the resistance was passive. The intention was to increase this pressure as the campaign matured by throwing in greater numbers to the point where it would cause serious embarrassment to authorities, who would have difficulty in coping with so many breaches of the law. It was hoped that the campaign would somehow disrupt the administration and force the government to concede that the particular laws could no longer be implemented.[38] Some spokesmen seemed to believe that the government might be forced to suspend all discriminatory legislation. Most importantly, the campaign was intended to overcome fear of authority, build an oppositionist attitude among the black people and raise political consciousness to a higher level. Efforts were made to show that separate aspects of colour discrimination were part of a system of white domination and that freedom from these restrictions necessitated a struggle for nation liberation. Individual acts of defiance were often placed in a context of non-cooperation with the system as a whole, which was condemned as repressive and exploitative. However, the notion of breaking the system by means of non-cooperation was raised largely by implication (since the law prohibited overt references). Violence was condemned as unnecessarily provocative and as necessarily leading to polarisation of the races and to civil war.

At the same time, the Defiance Campaign was shown to be the consequence of the closing of all constitutional means for redress of just grievances. The campaign was presented as an extreme measure of last resort which would somehow force the government to relent.

History shows that the campaign succeeded in some of its objectives, the subjective ones, but failed on the main count.[39] Instead of bringing relief, repression intensified. And the whites were driven into a coalition united by the fear of losing their privileged position.[40] We also know that the tough counter-measures taken by the government caught the liberation movement off guard and that it had not prepared a line of retreat from the point of view of struggle tactics. It had not prepared for a new arena of struggle in the event of the repression that might have been foreseen. Furthermore, the syndrome of protest–repression continued throughout the 1950s without the development of new struggle strategies. No matter how high the mood of resistance rose, it was repeatedly beaten back by the government when it came to open confrontation.

But it would be wrong to focus on the immediate issues taken up by the ANC or on the methods of struggle and organisation for an explanation of the failure of what has been called the politics of protest.[41] The essential weakness lay rather in the woolly thinking on the nature of the structure of the system and the illusions this led to in the aims of these campaigns. Granted that the organisation and politicisation of the masses were a necessary primary objective; it was also incumbent on the leaders to think strategically.[42] There was always a reasonable expectation that matters would come to a head but there was lacking a concept of the actual transfer of power to guide the struggle in its more critical phases. Without such a concept mass militancy broke its spirit against the wall of the armed power of the state. It can be argued further that the conception of Conventional Democracy as held by the liberation movement was crippling for the advancement of the struggle. As long as the gaining of democratic rights was seen as an extension within the existing system, illusions were bound to flourish and the struggle methods would remain inadequate. Only the concept of Revolutionary Democracy with its emphasis on popular power and alternative power structures could lead to a more developed struggle form. In the South African case it would have inevitably led to a violent, that is armed, liberation struggle.

But in last resort, the failure of non-violence in South Africa was due to the system itself. White supremacy is based upon privilege and that privilege is given expression in a set of values that justifies the most cruel repression of those who challenge the system[43] and enables the rulers to turn to using ever greater legal powers and finally open violence against the protesters without incurring substantial criticism from within the white group itself.[44]

As Kuper pointed out, polarisation is based on opposed interests and antithetical values. 'The subject peoples deny legitimacy to the social order and the rulers respond with increasing repression ... There is no neutral ground of detachment from the struggle, which drives all strata into opposing camps.' The consequence is clear. 'If the society is polarised, then it may be reasonable to infer that political change will be abrupt, revolutionary, and presumably violent.'[45]

The benefit of hindsight enables us to come to the conclusion that the liberation movement did not draw the necessary inference from their experience that they should prepare for a struggle that would necessarily be revolutionary in every sense.

○○○

After the Defiance Campaign the liberation movement continued strenuously with campaign after campaign to build a mass base for political pressure on the government. These campaigns were non-violent as before, but they were nevertheless meant to arouse the militancy of the mass of black people and to strengthen grassroots organisation.

Conditions were far from easy for this kind of work, which was mainly in the open, and those who argue for 'openness' in principle[46] would have been persuaded otherwise in the South African setting. The period under review saw Congress exploit every conceivable opportunity for public campaigning. Thousands of meetings were held throughout the country, there were demonstrations and mass lobbies involving tens of thousands of people. There was the Treason Trial in 1956–61 with all the surrounding campaigns 'in defence of the leaders'. There was the famous Alexandra bus boycott when the population of one of the largest African townships in Johannesburg walked nine miles to work daily in a successful protest against a penny increase in fares. Yet, despite many mass demonstrations, nothing changed. Mass protest ran its full course till it was out of breath. The National Party government and its machine of repression clamped down ever more firmly and there was no sign that any substantial body of white opinion wanted it otherwise. South Africa was moving inexorably, albeit reluctantly, towards violent confrontation.

Non-Racial Policies
We now turn to four aspects which bear directly on the

subsequent transfer to violent action by the liberation movement. Two of these aspects are political: the polarisation of white and black, and the consolidation of white power; and two are tactical: the waning possibilities of 'open' activity, and the development of the 'underground' alternative.

Apart from the Black Republic period of the CP in the 1930s and the momentary exclusivist African nationalism of the ANCYL in the mid–1940s, these two sectors of the liberation movement staunchly stuck to non–racialism as the ultimate policy over a period of at least thirty years. This policy was embodied in all major political documents, not least in the Freedom Charter which opens with the statement 'South Africa belongs to all who live in it Black and White'.

Non–racialist democracy as a policy, however, did not eliminate African identity. During the whole of this period the ANC remained an exclusively African organisation and cooperation with Coloureds, Indians and whites was carried out as between their respective organisations. By the mid–1950s five organisations, representing the national groups and trade unions, were working together in the Congress Alliance led by the ANC. The CP had not yet reappeared on the scene though its members were active within these five organisations.

The non–racial democratic policy of the ANC must be seen in its proper light. It was an expression of political goals, a framework within which African liberation would be fought for, and it was clearly and unambiguously against conceptions like an independent African state, African separatism or even African domination. All nationalities were assumed to have equal rights, though being the largest group and the most oppressed, it was understood that the African people would constitute the most important section.

It will be seen therefore that the non-racial perspective of the ANC leadership was an important matter of principle.[47] Having suffered race discrimination themselves, they wanted no part in policies of African exclusivism. Some held this view from the position of a general democratic outlook; others, who held to a Marxist analysis of society, because they feared that an anti-white policy would distort the struggle into a cleavage based on colour instead of class, resulting in a society where white capitalists were replaced by black. The Marxists felt that black nationalism in an extreme form of anti-whiteism would divert the struggle from a positive, wide-ranging democratic movement involving people of all races (especially the Indian and Coloured minorities which are substantial, and also white revolutionaries) into a sectarian, purely African movement encouraging race hatred. Both groups feared that the adoption of a purely racial posture would lead to a bloodbath.

The influence of white liberals was also important in holding down African nationalism by engaging African leaders in a constant dialogue which seemed to hold a promise of significant political support, though this in fact never materialised. Another factor undercutting black exclusivism was the undoubted desire on the part of some African leaders to be accepted by whites as people who understood and accepted so-called 'civilised' Western values. These tendencies were enhanced by the continuing process of economic integration of black people into the white-dominated economy and the consequent increasing contacts across the colour line.

Most important, however, was the objective of the liberation movement to drive a wedge into the white camp to prevent white consolidation. It considered that a united white community would be a very formidable enemy indeed. Every effort was made by African leaders to meet with and persuade influential whites to make public gestures rejecting apartheid and oppose the Nationalist government. The white Congress of Democrats was set up to organise white opposition. Government on the other hand was well aware of the dangers of such tendencies and exerted tremendous pressure on liberal whites to hamper their activities and prevent the breakaway of a significant section of white opinion. In the long run intimidation won out and even those whites who would have preferred a less rigid system and whose minds were still open were driven into acquiescence or silence.

The role of the Communist Party as the only radical organisation without a colour bar was an important element in the maintenance of non-racial policies. The CP held an anomalous position in the liberation front. It had been banned in 1950 before the Alliance was set up formally, and since it was the only illegal body on the left it could not take its place around the table. No doubt some ANC leaders were content with this and there was no attempt to get round the difficulty and meet as organisations behind the scenes. Nevertheless, CP members belonged to all the Congress organisations, and since some of the top Congress leaders and outstanding cadres were also in the CP, it exercised considerable influence within the Alliance. It was the enforced 'hidden' participation of the CP in the Alliance that led to charges that ANC was unduly influenced by the CP and, in particular, by its more prominent white members. This complaint was made more credible by virtue of the fact that the CP had had a predominantly white Central Committee at the time it was banned. This gave an impression among Africans that the CP was basically a white organisation with a 'white' ideology. Many of these people continued to be active afterwards, and it may be assumed that their influence in the movement as a whole continued.

But the ANC rebutted the charges of undue influence vigorously, insisting that its policies were determined independently, and that African communist members of the ANC participated as individuals only. Furthermore, the ANC defended its alliance with the Congress of Democrats on the grounds of non-racial principle and as being in line with the goals of the Freedom Charter. By the mid-1950s African exclusivism was condemned, charges of race hatred denied, and the platforms of Congress meetings reflected the active participation of all races. In some branches and areas, however, notably Sophiatown and the Eastern Cape (probably the most militant in the country), there was a sharp edge of anti-white sentiment and a strong black populist current in the propaganda.

If some reservations remained in the ANC about the increasingly public cooperation with other races in the framework of the Congress Alliance, this was finally put aside after the arrests of the Treason Trial in 1956. All told, 156 leaders of all organisations were charged with conspiracy to overthrow the government and set up a 'communist' state. The trial consolidated the Congress Alliance, highlighted the very real commitment to the struggle of all the partners in the Alliance and brought out the general democratic aims of the movement.

What basis is there for the assertion, made even now, that whites undermined African nationalism and exerted excessive influence on the liberation movement as a whole? Is there any truth in the allegation that communists, especially white communists, strove to play down African nationalism in an effort to press a non-racial and socialist programme? Did white participation at the highest levels lead to an emasculation of ANC policies?[48] Did the growing integration of the Congress Alliance and its stress on non-racial democracy undermine its potential black support?[49] These questions are controversial and remain a matter of contention in South Africa today.

Critics of the Congress Alliance have said that the prominent whites in the movement were not fully committed to the struggle by virtue of their affluence and comfortable life-style. It has also been suggested they could not but fall down in their leadership roles since they were not part of the oppressed and could not possibly interpret what the masses were saying. One particularly hostile critic has said that they had a subconscious 'will to fail'. These criticisms require an answer, not least because they help clarify the nature of the choices open to the liberation movement.

Certainly there were many persistent white liberals who were constantly striving to influence ANC leaders in the direction of caution and dialogue. But there were whites of a different stamp, communists and committed democrats, who were active within the liberation movement. Can the charge of diluting the struggle be made about them? They were certainly influential through the CP and the Congress of Democrats and their very direct involvement in the action. They could hardly be faulted on the grounds of their commitment. At most it may be said that they (together with many blacks) strove to play down African nationalism in the Alliance in order to develop a non-racial democratic programme.

There was also an implicit assumption in the Alliance

that all racial groups could play a somewhat equal role, and the necessity of always ensuring the leading role of Africans was sometimes forgotten. Perhaps the participation of whites in the movement did inhibit the development of self-confidence and leadership qualities among Africans, as some people suggest, since white South Africans, like intellectuals in any movement, tend to work with greater confidence, using their talents and expertise with effect. Perhaps – though the evidence is far from conclusive.

What could be argued more convincingly is that the mere presence of whites at the top layers of the movement was misunderstood by the masses and that they were not able to identify wholly with a movement which gave such status to members of the ruling race. The demand for national liberation for the black people must have sounded strange coming from white South Africans. Perhaps this is taking a narrow view, underestimating the ability of the man-in-the-street to comprehend that there were some whites who had broken with their own kin and thrown in their lot with the oppressed.

Three points can be made with confidence. First, there have been a good number of white South Africans totally committed to the struggle and prepared to give life itself for their convictions. And this is no flash in the pan. There is a long tradition among white radicals, going back many decades, of involvement and commitment in the struggle for liberation in South Africa. The analysis and questioning in this article must not be seen as an

67

attempt to minimise their contribution.

Second, no matter how exclusive a black movement may be, it cannot for long help but seek the cooperation of white sympathisers. The moment a movement goes beyond words, it is bound by the dynamics of struggle to welcome the participation of anyone, including those who desert the enemy ranks.

Third, since the primary aspect of the struggle in South Africa is the struggle for black liberation from white domination, the movement must be in fact, and it must be seen to be, led by black leaders. The primacy of African leadership and solidarity is not a matter of sentimentality, or of sleight of hand; it is an essential requirement if the movement is to maintain its credibility with the mass of the people, and if it is to lead them correctly.

Though it would be a narrow view which urged that a leader has to be poor to understand the social dynamics of poverty, one must concede that a white intellectual whose life-style and daily experience is remote from that of the oppressed has some difficulty in formulating policies of struggle for the oppressed. One might draw a parallel from the policies of communist parties which insist that workers should constitute a majority of the leadership. By extension of this principle, most of the important policy-makers in a mature and effective liberation movement must be from the oppressed group, and this is particularly important where, as in the South African case, the differences between the two groups are so great.

The most that can be made of the question regarding excessive white influence on policies is that the movement may have been over-anxious to present a non-racial image, thereby losing some of its impact as a force for the liberation of Africans, the major component of the struggle.

In any event, non-racialism did not prove to be an acceptable alternative to the white ruling class – and this is hardly surprising. By and large, whites acquiesced in the repression of the liberation movement and this cannot be merely ascribed to irrational fears of a bloodbath. It seems that white South Africa was far more careful with its arithmetic than has often been suggested.[50]

Looked at coldly, the propositions of the ANC were not at all in the immediate short term interests of white South Africa. The proposal of 'one man, one vote' would have resulted in an immediate African majority in parliament; the demand for the removal of the economic barriers would have led to an influx into the white areas of petty African traders who would have undercut small white businessmen. Relaxation in job restrictions would have meant the rapid displacement of expensive white labour by cheap, semi-skilled but keen black labour; removal of the Pass Laws would have led to the massive influx of rural African poor into the cities where white privilege of every kind would have been under attack. In short, the bastion of white privilege and supremacy in every sphere was at issue, and this was not going to be surrendered easily.

From the viewpoint of blacks, the demand for equal rights was minimum. It was the only way to break the monopoly of white privilege and power. For this reason the lines were very clearly drawn, and hopes of splitting the whites on an issue of fundamental principle were unrealistic.

Many liberal writers on South Africa have suggested that the ANC was putting forward a 'liberal' programme of non–racialism, while others have used the terms 'bourgeois democracy'.[51] But in a systematic presentation of the programme of the movement in the 1950s, Moses Kotane spoke of a People's Democracy and this was the term used in various lectures distributed at the time of the Congress of the People (1955) when the Freedom Charter was launched.

We can adopt one of two positions. Either the demands for equality and so on were so broad that they could be interpreted in any way members of Congress wished – and there was certainly a wide range of ideological positions held within Congress – or the demands of the movement did in fact represent a coherent programmatic position. Some have suggested that since the removal of the colour bar was so fundamental, it would set in motion such a social upheaval that the purely political aspect, in terms of votes and majorities, would inevitably be accompanied or followed by far more fundamental changes in the base, namely in the relations of production. They also argued that since the petty-bourgeois section of the African people is relatively small, the shock troops of change would be workers and peasants who would not stop the process at a point where a black bourgeoisie would replace the white. On this analysis it is not necessary and is needlessly divisive for the ANC to articulate its ideology more specifically. Unfortunately, these questions have not been hammered out within the ANC and the issues are still wide open.

The point that needs emphasis is that even though the demands for equality made in the 1943 ANC constitution were far-reaching and potentially revolutionary, these demands were at first presented as though they could be won (even gradually) within the existing institutional framework. Only later, when the concept of People's Democracy was raised, and later still, when the struggle assumed the sharpest form, was the programme of the ANC seen as a basis for a new state form, however vague its outline. This means that when it is suggested that there was a reformist element present, the reference is primarily to the posture and perspectives of the movement and only secondarily to the programmatic formulation of principles. It could be argued conclusively that any demand for equal rights was revolutionary in South Africa, but this would not prove that the movement was revolutionary. Its demands would have to be concretised in a perspective of revolutionary praxis. This was soon to develop.

PART TWO
The Transfer to Violence

There can be little doubt that the campaigns of the 1950s politicised large numbers of the oppressed, particularly those in the urban areas. But toward the close of the decade it was becoming apparent that mass support for Congress campaigns was falling off. No doubt the government's systematic use of bannings, banishment and other administrative repressive means was having some effect, since public work was becoming increasingly circumscribed. Since the policy was to use only open political action, a sense of frustration began to enter into the situation, especially among the unorganised supporters of Congress.

The relative inactivity, at least in the urban areas, led some sympathisers to question the possibility of change at all. Julius Lewin opened a debate in *Africa South* with an article 'No Revolution Round the Corner' reflecting his general pessimism.[52] Replying, Michael Harmel, a leading member of the CP and Congress movement, argued that the poverty and oppression of blacks was gross, driving them into protests and demonstrations which were all working towards revolutionary change. Harmel insisted that 'revolution need not involve violence. There have been plenty of examples in history where a combination of factors has been compelling enough to make a ruling class give way for urgent and overdue changes, without dragging the people through the agony of civil war.' (Two years later Harmel was one of the first to admit that violence was inescapable for revolutionary change.)

Yet apart from the apparent reluctance of the urban masses to participate in large numbers in Congress campaigns, there were signs in the countryside that a new momentum of a different order was building up. The immediate issues behind the eruptions of militant and often violent action on a large scale varied, but they were all related to the new oppressive restrictions being enforced by the government and its paid agents, the chiefs and headmen in the reserves (now called homelands).

The reserves consist of eight 'national units' of about seven million people and add up to some 13% of South Africa's land surface. Each of the main units has some form of government-sponsored tribal authority which is supervised by white civil servants seconded from Pretoria. The reserve economies have long been undermined by the draining-off of able-bodied labour for work in the white economy, and by overcrowding which has brought productivity below subsistence levels. Per capita income has been declining for a long time and 74% of the land is eroded.[53] Poverty is widespread and deep while the infant mortality rate is phenomenal. The reserves are but rural slums ruled by indifferent officials using the harshest of regulations.

In 1957 the grinding mills of poverty and official interference brought matters to a head. African women in the Bahurutshe Reserve in the Zeerust area demonstrated against the issuing of pass books by officials. Hundreds of women burned their books and a large number were arrested. Migrant workers from Zeerust working in Johannesburg returned on the weekends to attend tribal meetings, which revealed the existence of two factions: supporters of government-oriented chiefs and their opponents. Unrest continued for about a year, often flaring up into violence. Huts were burned and there were numerous cases of assault, building up into open warfare. The tribal courts imposed severe punishments. The police were very active and on one occasion used a military aircraft to disperse a crowd of women. About 200 persons were charged with offences ranging from murder and arson to carrying on prohibited political activity.[54]

Even more serious trouble developed in the Sekhukhuneland Reserve over the introduction of Bantu Authorities and cattle-culling schemes. Here again there was near civil war with numerous assaults and assassinations. When, in May 1958, the police attempted to make some arrests general rioting broke out and armed peasants attacked government agents. The police returned in strength making more than 330 arrests. Many were given life sentences, others periods of ten years imprisonment for public violence, assault or arson. The Chief of the region was banished to a remote area hundreds of miles away, where he lived in isolation and near starvation for a number of years.

In mid-1959 rioting occurred in the outlying towns and countryside throughout Natal. The catalyst in the rural areas was the extension of influx control to women and trouble over dipping tanks. Women held meetings and processions, large numbers of dipping tanks were destroyed, fires were started on white farms, and for some days there was panic among whites in various country towns. About 600 women were arrested, followed by the inevitable trials and imprisonment. Other violent incidents occurred in urban and rural areas throughout the country, with loss of life on all sides.

The most dramatic revolt took place in Pondoland during 1959–60.[55] The imposition of Bantu Authorities (a form of tribal local government) and its high-handed implementation by government stooges among the chiefs led to bitter strife. A Hill Committee was formed to lead the resistance, which rapidly became widespread. Muriel Horrell writes: 'Chiefs who supported government policies were attacked and in some cases murdered; huts were burned; the chiefs concerned appointed home guards who in some cases conducted retaliatory attacks; fences and other betterment works were destroyed. For many months pro-government chiefs went in fear of their lives. In some cases the police opened fire to disperse angry mobs, a tragic occurrence took place at Ngquza Hill near Bizana in June 1960 when eleven Africans were shot dead and thirteen wounded. Africans murdered two chiefs, two headmen, four councillors, and seventeen commoners; and another three Africans were killed as a result of police action.[56]

The revolt was ultimately crushed by a massive military intervention by the crack Black Watch Brigade, which surrounded the region, cut off all roads and then went in to smash all opposition.

Sharpeville and Regrouping Underground

The significance of these events in the rural areas was to a certain extent lost on the country as a whole. Even in the ranks of the liberation movement, which were excessively urban-oriented, the rural rebellions were not fully understood. The movement continued to focus its attention primarily on urban areas with most of the work confined to African townships.

Every town and city in South Africa has its own satellite township for the African work force. In the rural white towns they may be only a thousand or two, but in Johannesburg there is a massive complex of townships for nearly a million Africans. They are controlled by a large black and white force of police and municipal guards who oversee the administration of multiple regulations on rents, housing, visitors and almost every aspect of life.

In the past some townships, which grew up in the period of rapid industrial expansion during and after the war, enjoyed a certain degree of freedom from municipal control. In Alexandra Township, for instance, there was a strong communal spirit which resisted officialdom to the point where police did not dare patrol the streets even in vans. When tension was high, the roads were barricaded, police and officials were attacked with stones and bottles and fired on by armed gangs, which operated numerous rackets inside and outside the township. In a sense Alexandra was the first 'no-go' area in a South African township, and not unnaturally it was a strong base for ANC organisation.

What was disquieting in the closing years of the 1950s was that even in these townships active support for the movement was slipping away. A magnificent bus boycott, which made a national impact, was carried out in Alexandra Township itself, but taken as a whole the urban scene was not encouraging. Within the Congress Alliance there was a growing recognition that the masses were expecting a more militant lead than had been provided in the past. The Congress movement therefore decided on a mass resistance campaign to mobilise people against passes, which were pressing on Africans more than ever. However, the Pan Africanist Congress (a splinter organisation) anticipated the campaign[57] and in March 1960 organised a series of peaceful demonstrations outside police stations. (PAC disavowed violence at this time.)[58] The demonstrations resulted in the shootings at Sharpeville where 69 Africans were killed and 178 wounded, an event which triggered off the most intense political reaction. It led to a wholly successful Day of Mourning called by Chief Luthuli during which black South Africans stayed at home. Those who did not were attacked on their return to African townships at night, and here and there some public buildings were set alight. On 30 March some 30,000 Africans marched on the city of Cape Town under PAC leadership. On the same day the government declared a State of Emergency and detained 20,000 people. In Durban thousands of Africans marched from the township Cato Manor demanding the release of the detainees, who now numbered 11,279 Africans, 90 Asians, 36 Coloureds and 98 whites. The Citizen Force and Skiet Commandos (all white) were mobilised and deployed around the towns.

In all, between 21 March and 19 April 1960, 83 civilians and 3 policemen lost their lives in various actions, and 365 civilians and 59 policemen were injured.[59] During the emergency the ANC set up a skeleton underground organisation which was able to keep the organisation intact. The CP issued its first public leaflet announcing its existence.

The shootings at Sharpeville marked a turning point. Not only did they highlight the wanton violence of the oppressors but they removed any belief in the possibility of making a dent in the system by means of protest politics alone. Following so quickly after the crushing of the Pondo Revolt by purely military action, the Sharpeville and Langa shootings broke the belief that a non-violent solution was possible.[60] Furthermore, the mass arrests and detentions that followed the declaration of a State of Emergency, and the holding of thousands of people without trial, destroyed any hope that the legal system could be used to halt police repression. It was evident that the long chain of legal victories in the courts had now been broken and that government had finally managed to impose a rule by direct police terror, brooking no hindrance from legal obstacles. It was also clear that the previous decade had been used effectively by the National Party to remove its white critics from the army, police and administration and consolidate its hold on all the organs of power. The pockets of opposition among the whites were rendered inactive, although the opposition press was still allowed some room for criticism beneath the heavy blanket of censorship.

To the leaders of the liberation movement it was now obvious that the state had been geared to maximum repression and that white public opinion supported it fully in this role. The foundation for transfer from non-violence to armed struggle was being laid.

Gene Sharp has argued that it is wrong to think that because all conventional political efforts and non-violent action have been forbidden, violence should now be used. 'Increasing government repression now makes it much more difficult to organize non-violent resistance especially openly than it was in 1952. But it is no easier to organize violent resistance.'[61] Sharp is missing the point. The reason for the abandonment of non-violent action, including strike action, was the qualitatively different character assumed by the state apparatus. Not only was it not conceivably open to conversion, but coercion had to be maximised if there was even to be a possibility of success. The transfer to violence was not due to impatience or petulance. A new stage had been reached in confrontation and this meant raising the level of attack to a much sharper form. This necessity was being grasped intellectually at the higher levels of the liberation movement, but it was also understood at the base from sheer practical experience.

Any kind of mass action or protest was becoming increasingly difficult to organise whether openly or for that matter covertly. Public meetings were always attended by police with tape recorders and the smallest legal transgression resulted in prosecution. Worse, speakers were arrested even where there were no legal grounds and the crowd turned upon by baton-wielding police. Protest meetings which met with violence from the authorities seemed to lose all point: the imperviousness to complaint indicated very clearly that action of a more drastic nature was needed.

In addition, organisation was made increasingly difficult. Even branch meetings were invaded by the police and, when the ANC was banned in 1960, government went all out to make this effective. The ANC, however, decided that it would not, as a matter of principle, accept the banning and would not wind up its organisation. It was important, they felt, to maintain a defiant posture so that there would be no demoralisation among the masses. But the problem of maintaining an 'open' form of activity in conditions of illegality was no small matter.

Top-level meetings were difficult to organise and the documents of the organisation were constantly being seized. It became more and more difficult to maintain a national network working in concert and keeping proper regular contact. New organisational forms had to be found.

The harassment of the ANC even in its legal days had been intense. There were numerous arrests of banned people who broke their restrictions, of activists who were engaged in what was technically legal but was considered subversive and dangerous by the police. The disruption of organisation was persistent and damaging. Yet somehow the work went on, and even flourished as the political climate was so favourable. But after the banning of the ANC, police surveillance became so tight that work in the open was well-nigh impossible. It was the State of Emergency that forced the movement underground, thereby revealing a new range of possibilities. Prior to 1960 activists in the liberation movement, of whom a large number were banned, operated on two levels, open and covert. They sat in offices behind desks and produced legal publications, but they also met other banned personnel in private. While this system made it possible to combine legal and illegal work effectively, it also gave leads to the police. With the declaration of a State of Emergency this system was changed. The centre of operations was now moved underground and it proved to be not only possible but more efficient, since underground personnel were in hiding and more free from police surveillance. The underground proved in many ways to be safer than the semi-legal system, though it also presented many problems.

What needs to be emphasised here, however, is that a movement that sets up an underground apparatus has moved very far indeed from the position it held formerly. It requires a total reorientation in political outlook. The underground activist is a social outcast isolated in his network of close associates. He must shed his remaining illusions of political participation as an ordinary citizen. For the moment, going underground implies the total rejection of the existing political system. It is wholly subversive in its intention and cannot conceal this fact. Contact between ruler and ruled is broken and the activists are consequently subjected to even more extreme forms of repression, including torture and detention, to enable the police to break into the underground network. The underground is the sine qua non of violent struggle while it also creates the basis of revolutionary power as an alternative to the existing power structure. The underground symbolises the transfer from the concept of Conventional Democracy to that of Revolutionary Democracy. It enables the creation of a new army of militants who live in isolation from the ordinary political pressures of the rest of the population, and who can therefore adopt a posture that is as different from the conventional as is the guerrilla from the politician.

The transfer from open, legal or semi–legal protest politics to the underground struggle was not an easy one in South Africa. It required a fundamental revision of thinking, posture and lifestyle for the leaders and activists in the liberation movement, which was difficult to make; and inevitably there were some who never made it.

For instance, when the State of Emergency was lifted in August 1960 and the detainees released, some crucial sections of the underground structure were abandoned and people returned to their earlier vulnerable places.

It seems that the movement was impelled to go forward for one more major, if non–violent, effort in the open before it could come to terms irrevocably with the need for a violent alternative; this took the form of the All-In African Conference in Pietermaritzburg on 25 March 1961.

Nelson Mandela made the main speech, attacking the government for its decision to set up a 'White Republic' and called for the convening of a National Convention based on universal franchise. The resolution stated, 'We declare that no Constitution or form of government decided without the participation of the African people who form an absolute majority of the population can enjoy moral validity or merit support either within South Africa or beyond its borders.'

The conference called for nationwide demonstrations and appealed to Africans not to cooperate or collaborate with the 'proposed South African Republic or any other form of government which rests on force to perpetuate the tyranny of a minority'. Mandela then went into hiding to lead a national strike.[62] The movement was carried along, refusing to recognise that the police state always referred to in speeches really existed. Hundreds of leaders had been banned, the organisations were banned, as were meetings and most forms of public work. There was ample evidence that the state apparatus was being sharpened for the counter push, but the movement had not yet abandoned its open style of operation entirely. The three-day strike began with considerable support but the police reacted with great vigour, arresting pickets and intimidating the hesitant in house-to-house raids. Employers and the daily press issued sharp warnings of dismissal and worse. By the third day it was fading.

With the strike broken, the movement was left to reassess its policies in a thoroughgoing manner. Smashing of the strike by brutal police action confirmed finally that open, peaceful mass demonstrations were no longer possible. Even when people were prepared to risk their jobs and face arrest on various technical infringements, the scale of police force made it well-nigh impossible to break through. And the memory of the Sharpeville massacre was still very fresh. Open resistance seemed naive and even irresponsible as the movement could provide no protection for defenceless workers.

At the same time it was recognised that isolated and spontaneous acts of violence were of no value and often counter-productive. There had already been numerous cases of people taking action against police and against traitors, and not only in the countryside. In the African complexes in Johannesburg scabs returning from work on the evening of a strike had been assaulted and even fired on by young unorganised men, who had also acted against isolated police patrols. But a national struggle could not be built on this sort of action.

The strike brought home to the movement and the oppressed people as a whole that the army and police in South Africa would stop at nothing in a showdown. It was an important reminder that, unlike in Europe or other countries, the army in South Africa is recruited not from the working class or peasantry, but from the privileged white workers and farmers, and they would give no quarter in a confrontation.

There was now a widespread belief that the violence of the authorities had to be reciprocated by the movement.[63] In some sections of the movement the conviction was growing that there would be a loss of morale unless ways were found to demonstrate that the oppressed were not without capacity to retaliate. Blacks had to show that white rulers were still vulnerable and could be hurt. More, if the ANC was to maintain its place it must be seen to be working to a plan which was leading to total struggle.

There was also a reluctant recognition that the effect of the national strike was to unite white opinion and strengthen the hand of the Nationalist government.[64] The line was being drawn ever more sharply between black and white. Most important of all, the belief was growing that a revolutionary and necessarily violent struggle would have to be waged to break the apartheid state.[65]

In retrospect it may seem remarkable how slow this idea was to attain ascendancy in the liberation movement. And even when the need for violence was recognised, how tardy the implementation was of the first steps. But we must recognise that with constant harassment of the leadership it was difficult to conduct the kind of cool reassessment and reorganisation that were needed for a major change in direction.

In an interesting paper called 'Reason and Violence', Roy Edgley has discussed the futility of engaging in argument with a person who has closed his mind to argument itself. Only some form of coercion then remains. But the transition may be difficult, particularly when the person who considers himself the victim believes firmly in the validity of argument as a means of settling disputes. The analogy holds good in the South African case. On the one hand the government had long relied entirely on force to maintain the white state intact, while the oppressed had engaged in numerous efforts at dialogue and protest to bring about change. Recognition that neither would do came hard and implementation even more so, especially for men who had spent a lifetime in open non-violent politics.

The difficulty lay in part in the isolation from the rest of the world, which all South Africans suffer and which, because of the banning of literature and travel restrictions, the leaders of the liberation movement suffered more than others. Increased world contact would have revealed new options much earlier.

At the turn of the 1960s Black Africa was rapidly gaining independence from direct colonial rule but their freedom was won without violence. There was no model here for the South African movement to follow. In Algeria, the only other country with a large white minority of the settler type, the struggle was swimming in blood and not encouraging. Only Che Guevara's book on guerrilla warfare seemed to suggest a new model of struggle. But conditions and traditions were very different in the two countries, and the lessons of Cuba were not easily applied. Mandela himself spent much of his time in hiding reading Clausewitz and similar works, but the working out of a wholly new strategy and tactics was bound to take time, particularly as police harassment was constant and steadily increasing. Police surveillance was vast and they were in the favourable position of knowing all the key figures in the movement and the organisational structure down to branch level.

It was also soon recognised that there was a great lack of full-time trained cadres at the crucial middle level. Men who had performed magnificently as local leaders at branch or regional level in open conditions were not always suitable for the rigours of the underground and for violent methods. Many lacked necessary skills like driving a car, using tools and implements, and the numerous other skills that the freedom fighter needs. Nevertheless, the pressures for a new initiative were overwhelming. A seemingly revolutionary situation was developing, violence was breaking out in town and country, political consciousness had never been higher, and the liberation movement had to move – and in a new direction.

Sabotage and the White State Focused

The form of violence decided upon was a campaign of sabotage of government buildings and installations and a core of men was created for the purpose. It was hoped that sabotage would have a profound demonstration effect, raising morale, seizing the initiative from the government and turning the movement away from the old-style protests. The sabotage was, as Bram Fischer told the court, directed primarily at symbolic targets. The first acts were carried out on a symbolic day too – it was Dingaan's Day, the day when white conquest was finally established.[66]

The sabotage attacks were explained in leaflets issued in the name of a new organisation linked to the Congress Alliance called Umkhonto we Sizwe (Spear of the Nation). The leaflet said that Umkhonto was 'formed by Africans. It includes in its ranks South Africans of all races and that it would carry on the struggle for freedom and democracy by new methods, which are necessary to complement the actions of the established national liberation organisations … It will be the fighting arm of the people against the government and its policies of race oppression … We of Umkhonto we Sizwe have always sought – as the liberation movement has sought – to achieve liberation without bloodshed and civil clash. We do so still. We hope even at this late hour that our first actions will awaken everyone to a realisation of the disastrous situation to which the Nationalist [government] policy is leading. We hope that we will bring the government and its supporters to their senses before it is too late, so that both government and its policies can be changed before matters reach the stage of civil war.'

The sabotage attacks were enough to throw the government and the white ruling class as a whole into a frenzy. Though it took a few months for the government to organise its repressive agencies on an even higher level, and also to pass necessary validating legislation, when counter-measures came they were very tough.

Umkhonto was not alone in the field. Other sabotage organisations were the African Resistance Movement, formed by young white leftists and disillusioned members of the Liberal Party, and Poqo, the military wing of PAC, which was also founded in 1961. Poqo criticised Umkhonto for diluting African nationalism by admitting non-Africans and so the feud between the two mother bodies was carried over into the battle areas.[67]

Poqo was primarily active as a terrorist organisation. Evidence in court was that Poqo had killed three African policemen and a white man between March 1962 and February 1963. Poqo seems to have been responsible for the action in Paarl on 21 November 1962 when a police station was attacked, some shops burned and two white civilians killed. Five Africans died from police bullets and some 400 were arrested. Poqo was also involved in several attempts on the life of the now Prime Minister of the Transkei, Chief Kaiser Matanzima, a most unpopular man, hated for his violent suppression of all opposition and for collaborating with government and imposing its harsh measures in the reserve.

The Minister of Justice revealed in parliament on 12 June 1963 and 10 June 1964 that by the latter date 202 members of Poqo had been found guilty of murder, 12 of attempted murder or conspiracy to murder, 395 of sabotage, 126 of leaving the country illegally, and 820 of lesser crimes.[68] The scale of activity by all organisations is shown by the figure of 2,169 arrested under security laws in 1963. In addition to the persons charged, about 1,000 were detained under the Ninety-Day law.

It can be seen that the sweep of sabotage was considerable. It was used in town and country and by all the liberation movements. Yet it failed to ignite the prairie fire as many had hoped. While sabotage provided government with every excuse for unleashing a brutal wave of terror, it failed to mobilise the mass of people, who were caught by surprise. The black population welcomed the actions but showed little willingness to undertake similar acts spontaneously when called on to do so. This is hard to explain but it may be that the techniques used were too strange and difficult. But it is also likely that they had not been shown how isolated acts of sabotage were relevant to bringing about the downfall of the government. Sabotage remained the weapon of an elite corps in the liberation movement. As a consequence, sabotage had the effect of isolating the organised movement from the mass who felt unable to join in this new phase or even to defend the actionists when they were seized.[69]

Many were inevitably caught and forced, under systematic torture, to give away their contacts. Here, too, the movements revealed their unpreparedness. Having talked of fascism for a decade and more, the movements were nevertheless caught by surprise when the police behaved like fascists. Under torture, many victims found to their regret that they knew too much and that the police knew that they knew. The process of extraction of information was carried out in all its horror of vicious torture, murder and suicide. Remorselessly the police uncovered the networks and suppressed the organisations. Those who were not caught either went into hiding or fled abroad.

Looked at as a single phase of the struggle, it must be said that the sabotage campaign was abortive. While most members of the liberation movement would agree that the turn to violence was necessary and historically correct, the actual form of the campaign led down the road to disaster. It has been claimed that sabotage lifted the psychological shackles of legalism and of respect for white authority,[70] and that if the movement had not taken these steps it would not have survived politically.[71] In later years explanations for the setbacks suffered included 'mistakes of insufficient vigilance and inadequate organisation' and 'security lapses'.[72]

In the last analysis, however, what is important is that the sabotage campaign failed on the main count – it did not raise the level of action of the masses themselves. Although it seems that the masses supported and even welcomed the resort to force, they could find no way of joining in and expressing their support. They were left on the threshold, frustrated bystanders of a battle being waged on their behalf. Perhaps the over-sophisticated methods used in sabotage were themselves the consequence of the political outlook of the movement. As the leaflet of Umkhonto suggests, sabotage was seen as another vehicle for protest, and not as the first shots of a protracted struggle in which the masses had to play a crucial part. Instead of using highly technical gadgetry, the movement might have begun with the simplest methods, which would have been easily assimilated in a country where 'the population' is friendly and widely dispersed, while the authority is easily identified and spread thinly over the country as a whole. The essential thing at this stage was raising the level of struggle, step by step, in the words of Le Duan,[73] and if the assessment that the people were deeply disturbed by Sharpeville and subsequent events was correct, then the more effective methods were those that the masses could use too. It has often been said that the very deep involvement of the Vietnamese peasants was due to the simplicity of the weaponry in the earlier days, and it would seem that the parallel is appropriate.

As sabotage mounted, so the tone of propaganda of the ANC and Umkhonto altered. The African character of the movement was highlighted and the white state was focused sharply; in a leaflet issued around May 1963 the ANC said: 'The South African people are at war with Verwoerd. Twelve million people [the number of Africans, Indians and Coloureds at the time] will be slaves no longer ... To destroy Verwoerd we must destroy the instruments of white power ... How are we to smash them? With planned, strategic violence. Already scared, the whites are on the lookout ... We say that just as Africans bear the brunt of oppression under the white state, so will the white state be broken by the main force of African people. But this is no reason, we say, to reject comrades of other races whom we know are ready to fight with us, suffer and, if need be, die.'

In other statements Umkhonto said, 'Umkhonto is for activists. We have struck against the white state more than 70 times ... Umkhonto has powerful allies. The African states and the democratic world are four-square behind us. We have allies among other races in South Africa.' In 1963, when five white civilians were killed in the Transkei by alleged Poqo militants, the ANC issued a statement headed, 'After the Transkei killings – Listen white man.' And it went on, 'Political violence has become the South African way of life. Why? What can be done to stop it? ... Like the raid on Paarl last year, when seven people died, the motive is a massive political wrong, fury, frustration and contempt for what whites do'. 'Black, Coloured and Asian are sick to death of white supremacy. Sabotage erupts every other week throughout the country, now here, now there. The whites are turning vicious and panicky.'

And in a major policy document, 'The People Accept the Challenge of the Nationalists', dated 6 April 1963, the ANC National Executive said: 'The government will certainly be more ruthless than it has been, it already considers itself at war and is fighting a desperate battle. Every European citizen has been called to defend white supremacy. Whites have been called upon to sacrifice not only time and money but life itself.

It would be criminal on our part not to prepare the

Africans throughout the country on a similar scale. No one can afford to be neutral in this situation ... The times have changed, we must make only one call, WE DEMAND FREEDOM OR DEATH, there can be no middle course.'[74]

These quotations seem to indicate that the exigencies of the situation were now beginning to sharpen the policies of the ANC in two directions. The 'whiteness' of the oppressor was no longer minimised (and talk of rights for all went by the board) and a protracted civil war was implied even when not directly expressed.

Catastrophe at Rivonia

The sabotage campaign had the effect of polarising black and white loyalties and sharply increasing repression. Meanwhile the ANC and Umkhonto took up the task of planning widespread armed action.

Nelson Mandela and a small group of organisers began a drive to recruit into Umkhonto. The proposed structure was similar to the M-plan previously used by ANC for its volunteer corps, which set up cells with group leaders in a tight network in African townships.

An important policy statement was issued by the Central Committee of the Communist Party in April 1963. The statement said that things were coming to a head in the country and that while legal channels of political activity were being closed, 'the oppressed masses are turning to methods that are illegal and non-peaceful'. It pointed out that violent outbreaks were becoming more common and that many of these were local, spontaneous reactions by a harassed people. The statement urged that unplanned local actions should be discouraged and that what was needed was 'organized and planned mass self-defence and resistance'. It called for 'No desperation, no adventurism, but firm, resolute and revolutionary action'. Every local issue must be linked with the political issue of destroying white power, but that correct policies were insufficient. There must be adequate machinery to convey it to the people, and it warned that 'Failure to take necessary organisational steps would lead to a dangerous gap opening between the people and their leaders'. On the situation as a whole, the statement said, 'Verwoerd and Vorster are steadily turning the country into an armed camp, ruled by decree and martial law. They are heading for civil war.' It emphasised that if the government persisted with the present course, 'the only effect can be that the present outbreaks of sabotage and violence will develop into full-scale war, beginning with guerrilla operations in various parts of the countryside and culminating in an armed insurrection of the whole oppressed people throughout the country.'

At the same time, a group within Umkhonto was working on a plan named Operation Mayibuye. There is still some doubt whether the plan was ever properly adopted by the leadership of all the components of the movement, or whether this kind of consultation was possible in the prevailing conditions. The ambitious plan was nevertheless set in motion. In retrospect, it seems that if sabotage had not been able to establish itself as a continuing form of struggle because the method was too advanced and the organisation inadequate, then Operation Mayibuye was an even more dubious proposition. In a short time it led to the decimation of the movement.

The Plan opened with the following statement: 'The white state has thrown overboard every pretence of rule by democratic process. Armed to the teeth it has presented the people with only one choice, that is, its overthrow by force and violence. It can now truly be said that very little, if any, scope exists for the smashing of white supremacy other than by means of mass revolutionary action, the main content of which is armed resistance leading to victory by military means … We are confident that the masses will respond in overwhelming numbers to a lead which holds out a real possibility of successful armed struggle.'

The Plan envisaged 'organised and well–prepared guerrilla operations during the course of which the masses of the people will be drawn in and armed'. The document stated that there would be tremendous difficulties since the white state was powerful and the government could at least initially count on the support of three million whites. But South Africa was isolated in the world and the movement could expect 'almost unlimited assistance' from friendly governments.

'Although we must prepare for a protracted war, we

must not lose sight of the fact that the political isolation of South Africa from the world community of nations, and particularly the active hostility towards it from almost the whole of the African Continent and the socialist world, may result in such massive assistance in various forms that the state structure will collapse far sooner than we can at the moment envisage.

'In the initial period when for a short while the military advantage will be ours, the plan envisages a massive onslaught on pre-selected targets, which will create maximum havoc and confusion in the enemy camp and which will inject into the masses of the people and other friendly forces a feeling of confidence that here at last is an army of liberation equipped and capable of leading them to victory ... The time for small thinking is over because history leaves us no choice.'

The operational section of the Plan envisaged the 'simultaneous landing of four groups of 30 based on our present resources whether by ship or air, armed and properly equipped in such a way as to be self-sufficient in every respect for at least a month'. These groups would then select targets and attack. Prior to these arrangements guerrilla units would have been established in crucial areas. 'Our target is that, on arrival, the external force should find at least 7,000 men in the four main areas ready to join the guerrilla army in the initial onslaught.'

In the meantime the political wing of the movement was to 'arouse the people to participate in the struggles that are designed to create an upheaval throughout the country'. There was also to be a 'flood of leaflets by plane announcing the commencement of our armed struggle'.

The implementation of Operation Mayibuye cannot be dealt with here in any detail, nor is it necessary for our analysis. What must be said, however, is that once the main leadership was arrested at Rivonia in 1963, the Plan collapsed.

Many leaders and hundreds of the best cadres had been sent out of the country for training, and this seriously weakened the organisation at home. Those who remained were either jailed or immobilised. A serious miscalculation was the effectiveness of torture in extracting information leading to the uncovering of a sector of activists. As a result of arrests and the disclosures during prolonged interrogation, the underground was wiped out, and even the heroic effort of top cadres like Wilton Mkwayi, who returned after training abroad, was insufficient to renew the struggle.

There is an important lesson here. There can be no move towards the attack until a line of defence and retreat has been prepared. The line of defence lies in organisational arrangements which ensure that a leak to the police does not lead to the disclosure of a long chain of the organisation. The line of retreat refers to an adequate underground network of hiding places and routes for flight over nearby borders. It has become all too clear that without sound organisation at home, no developments abroad can really expect to lead to success, not least because of the absence of a friendly border.

Geographic Isolation

Unfortunately South Africa offers none of the terrain advantages associated with successful military operations by liberation movements elsewhere. Worse still, the country is situated at the tip of the African continent insulated from friendly African states by the buffer territories of Mozambique, Angola and Rhodesia. Swaziland, Botswana and Lesotho are also not very helpful, though they fall into a different category. At the same time, though the liberation movement in South Africa is deprived of friendly borders, there is not a great deal of solace for the white state either. The northern neighbours cannot be thought of as a rearguard for white South Africa – rather the reverse. The pressures to the north are bearing down toward the south, confirming the overwhelming view among white South Africans that they are firmly trapped in a geographic laager from which there is no escape. If serious trouble were to come, there would even be some difficulty in establishing a secure external base for imperialist support.

The consequences of remoteness are nevertheless very great for the South African liberation movement. An armed conflict without a nearby friendly border makes starting extremely difficult. Sustaining operations without safe supply lines is even more hazardous, and there is the additional problem of renewal of guerrillas. One has only to consider the importance of the North for South Vietnam, of China and the USSR for North Korea in the Korean war, of Tanzania and Zambia for Frelimo and the MPLA, of Guinea for PAIGC, of Tunisia for Algeria, for it to be evident that this is a crucial factor for the conduct of a protracted armed struggle. The outstanding exception is Cuba, where an insurgent force survived miraculously and went on to mobilise an insurrection. But that is an exception facilitated by the vacillation of the US. Certainly in the South African case, the problem of returning trained guerrillas from abroad and then keeping the action going is a formidable one. How Operation Mayibuye meant to overcome this is not known, but the fact that for some ten years a significant number of guerrillas have not been able to return is an indication that the proposal was unrealistic from the start.

The only serious attempt to return in force was in the Wankie and Eastern Front operations in Zimbabwe, when ANC and Zapu joined forces to enter Zimbabwe. In both those cases Rhodesian and South African security forces were able to intercept the guerrilla bands and prevent them marching further south. Some managed to enter Botswana, where they were arrested and imprisoned, while others returned over the Zambezi. The road to South Africa remained blocked. (Some of the participants in these incursions have argued that although it may be true now, it was not so at the time. They assert that the main error was the long delay and that if the guerrillas who were itching to go home to fight had been allowed to do so earlier when the Rhodesian forces were not yet prepared, they would have succeeded. The fact remains, however, that the road is now blocked.)

The Rhodesian Minister of Defence disclosed on 11 and 27 December 1968 that during the previous period more than 160 guerrillas (including 35 from South Africa) had been killed while others had been captured. On the Rhodesian side 12 were killed and 30 wounded, while 3 of the South African security forces died. It is likely that these figures are inaccurate since information from Rhodesian hospitals was that the government casualty lists were far greater.[75]

Much criticism has been levelled at the Rhodesian incursions. It has been said that the first band of 100 men was far too large, inevitably attracting the attention of the security forces. Again, the populace were not prepared to receive the guerrillas beforehand and the political organisation in the villages was lacking. Rhodesian security had terrorised the villagers into refusing to give food and water to the guerrillas, and on occasion Rhodesian African army men entered villages in the guise of guerrillas and, if they were not immediately betrayed, the village was punished terribly. In the end the villagers could not distinguish between genuine and fake guerrillas.[76]

These lessons have now been grasped fully. In the current 1973 incursions by Zapu and Zanu guerrillas there have been no concentrations of men and they have successfully exploited the broken terrain. The classic pattern of guerrilla warfare is now unfolding in that region and, if sustained, will bring much nearer the cooperative endeavours of the liberation movements in all southern Africa. The essential requirements for guerrilla action are local support, space for mobility, and supply lines for materials and trained men. As the struggle through southern Africa grows, so the different movements will be forced to help each other increasingly with routes through liberated territory and logistic arrangements of all kinds. This is already happening in the case of Zanu with Mozambique, and Swapo with Angola.

At the same time, South Africa's remoteness has a positive side too. A decade ago, particularly in the days of Nkrumah's extravagant claims that he would liberate all Africa, there were many who preferred waiting for liberation from the north to the rigours of self-reliance. This misplaced optimism is now gone and there is a sort of coherence about the situation which imposes the most hard-headed examination of the internal dynamics of the South African system as a basis for strategy in place of the easier option of outside intervention. It is often said that southern Africa is a single theatre of struggle – and so it is, with the successes of the armed struggles in Mozambique, Angola and Zimbabwe making an important psychological impact. But no movement can predict the stepping up of its struggle at home on successes elsewhere, particularly when these struggles are themselves likely to develop slowly and distances to the south are great.

There is an even greater imperative for focusing on South Africa itself. It is the heart of the white redoubt in the sub-continent and it is unthinkable that colonialism could be sustained in any of the neighbouring countries if South Africa itself was liberated. There is in any case an obligation on the movement to ease the passage of others by draining the strength of the octopus at the centre.

Nevertheless, what happens to the north is in many ways crucial. If the lines of communication of South Africa's armed forces become stretched over the whole of southern Africa, they will have serious logistic problems.[77] The area is vast, the population overwhelmingly black and the terrain to the north favourable for guerrilla warfare. Furthermore, the political consequences on an international level of South Africa's further military involvement will be serious. But, for the present, we must restrict our vision to the internal situation.

At this stage the major impact of armed battles to the north is psychological. The capacity of black guerrillas to hurt white troops and even to make a physical dent in white power is impressive. It cannot but generate a sense of confidence that the same will one day happen further south, and as a South African general astutely observed, confidence is all. He said: 'The objective for both sides in a revolutionary war is the population itself ... Military tactics and hardware are all well and good, but they are really quite useless if the government has lost the confidence of the people among whom it is fighting. And by the time their confidence has been lost, more armed force will cause the population to become antagonistic' (*The Star*, 27.1.1973).

'The people are the mountain,' said Cabral, and the problem is how they can generate the solidarity to enable them to dominate the plains. The answer lies in the development of a correct political line to which the mass of the people can respond readily and in the elaboration of a strategy and tactics to match. Progress in this area has been rather slow in coming over the past decade.

The Movement Abroad

From 1960, when the first leaders were sent out to rally international support, the movement abroad has grown steadily. Men like Oliver Tambo became the nucleus of a political mission (later called the External Mission) which encouraged anti-apartheid work around the world. Other leaders followed, charged with the specific task of organising an external armed force in the context of Operation Mayibuye. When Umkhonto collapsed inside the country, these men were faced with the need to deploy trained military cadres into camps in a number of countries. They were also responsible for the incursions into Zimbabwe already discussed. This function was later placed in the hands of the Revolutionary Council. a department of the National Executive of the ANC.

The External Mission placed a number of Chief Representatives in offices in various friendly countries and their work was coordinated from Morogoro in Tanzania, which housed the ANC External Mission headquarters. A vast amount of propaganda work has been carried out by this department, but the view is now growing within the movement itself that solidarity work and international questions have absorbed the exile leadership to the point where internal work has been neglected. There is the evident danger for any exile movement that it will become remote from home and that the possibilities of return will become even more unlikely. It has been said that in the hustle of international conferences and lobbying some leaders have temporarily forgotten that in the last analysis the only justification for an external organisation of South African freedom fighters lies in the work they do for the struggle at home and in preparation for their own return.

Some critics have blamed the weakening powers of an ageing leadership, which has sat in frustration thousands of miles away from the scene of action for ten years. Others have pointed to the bureaucratic structures that have grown up in exile. No one questions the importance of solidarity work, though it is often now accepted that it may become a bottomless pit for financial resources and manpower.

One of the difficulties is that once a large number of civilian members are organised abroad, the movement is tied down with work which is only tangential to the struggle. A similar difficulty has faced other liberation movements, and in the case of MPLA and Frelimo it was solved by disbanding the civilian structure and insisting that everyone become a trained fighter. Of course their geographic location and the advanced stage of their armed struggle made such a decision possible.

But what of the ANC's Revolutionary Council, which was charged with revitalising the organisation at home and with returning the trained army cadres? It is evident that success has been elusive, and the words of Cabral, 'The rice cannot be cooked outside the pot', come to mind. We can only refer here to public evidence of the return, which is available mainly from press reports of trials of men who have infiltrated from abroad. There have also been various propaganda campaigns carried out by some internal networks such as that run by Ahmed Timol, who was murdered by the Special Branch in 1972. But of military action inside South Africa there has been none thus far, though the Revolutionary Council has been grappling with the problem of getting going for some time.[78]

The most recent pronouncements of the external movement, however, indicate that the emphasis is once again moving away from immediate armed struggle and there is greater stress on rebuilding political structures at home. The urgent need seems to be for political organisers who can return home and take root among the masses rather in the way this was done in the early days by Cabral in Guinea. But the possibility of the infiltration of armed units has not been dismissed and the theoretical basis for this, the detonator theory which dominated the movement's thinking for some years, has not entirely been left behind. Its implementation, of course, depends on the possibility of returning armed men safely and setting them up with a chance of surviving.

Something needs to be said about the possibilities of concealing activists in the conditions of tight control obtaining in South Africa. Is the town more suitable than the country? Experience indicates that the possibilities are equal in town and country, though both are extremely difficult. In the country there is the advantage of a homogeneous people and more relaxed police surveillance. But this is offset by the existence of a stooge administration with its spies and agents everywhere. In the towns the density of population is an advantage as is the anonymity provided by any city area. But here the police vigilance is intense and raids on houses are frequent.

In South Africa it would be foolhardy to force dogmatically a pattern of organisation based on the Cuban or some other model when the situation is still so open.

A War of National Liberation

The terms of the conflict have now been laid down irrevocably and there can be no going back on violence and armed struggle. Though the first attempt in the early 1960s was crushed, there can be no turning back from the struggle for power that opened up then. Even while the wages issue now rises to the surface and other partial demands are manifested in a variety of struggle forms in the present stage, the major issue of power remains the crucial one.

I have tried to show that the system itself generates an impulse for a total solution. The absence of mediating political institutions, the sharp lines of class and colour cleavage, the nature of oppressive authority, all of these operate to focus on the extreme injustice of white rule. What is more, one cannot conceive of the intensification of any aspect of the struggle without seeing that the fundamental character of the system will become increasingly challenged.

Confirmation of increasing polarisation between the races comes in the responses of current African and black student opinion, which have begun to stress black solidarity as never before. Recently, there has emerged a militant black South African Students' Organisation (Saso) and the Black People's Convention, which include African, Indian and Coloured members, though Africans naturally predominate. These organisations have penetrated colleges and schools and have made a strong impact.

It is not only the students who are stressing 'blackness'. There have been serious rifts between white and black clergy, with black ministers staging several marches highlighting the discrimination against them. Black solidarity is stressed in the sports world where the government and white–controlled official bodies are constantly trying to introduce Uncle Toms and black terminology and postures are creeping into political and other literature in a way unknown before.

Does the increase of black consciousness mean that black South Africans are becoming anti–white in any sense of ultimate values, or is it a vehicle of struggle in reaction to white oppression? Doubtless there is a widespread loss of patience and a growing intolerance of white domination at all levels, including that of ordinary human contacts where white means privileged at every turn. But there is considerable evidence that blacks can still discriminate between friends and foes no matter what their colour, even while they take up a strong black consciousness position. In the liberation movement abroad, for instance, despite many strong pressures and temptations, the ANC leadership refuses to remove that sprinkling of white revolutionaries which has always distinguished this movement. Oliver Tambo, Acting President, put it this way in a speech on 26 June 1972: black consciousness, he said, posed tremendous problems at the theoretical level only. In action, barriers between the races would cease to exist and there would be room enough for fighters of all races.

In the document adopted at the Morogoro Conference in 1969 the ANC declared, 'The main content of the present stage of the South African revolution is the national liberation of the largest and most oppressed group – the African people. Among other things, it demands in the first place the maximum mobilisation of the African people as a dispossessed and racially oppressed nation. This is the mainspring and it must not be weakened. It involves stimulation and a deepening of national confidence, national pride and national assertiveness ... The national character of the struggle must therefore dominate our approach ... But none of this detracts from the basically national context of our liberation drive ... To blunt it in the interests of abstract concepts of internationalism is in the long run doing a service neither to revolution nor to internationalism.'[79]

In its internal propaganda at least, the ANC has increasingly come to use the language of blackness and, as I have shown, when the struggle was at its sharpest it focused on white rule, on the white state apparatus, and called for black solidarity. And this line is obviously correct, though it has not been followed consistently.

Black solidarity is the contemporary expression of the demand for national liberation. It is not pure demagogy, it has a social basis, and no political movement can succeed which fails to articulate this idea. To talk of national liberation, however, requires an answer to the questions, Which nation? And power for whom? It is not possible to present a systematic answer to this most thorny of theoretical questions of the South African revolution in this essay. Instead of looking at the issue theoretically for the moment, let us look at the practical aspects.

Considering the African people, what strata are included in the concept 'national liberation'? The size of the African industrial working class has been indicated earlier, as has the degree of urban African participation in the liberation struggle thus far. There can be no doubt about the future central role of African workers or of the advanced level of their political consciousness. Of rural Africans in the 'homelands' and on white farms, who may be classified as semi–peasants and rural proletarians, there can also be little doubt that their appalling conditions will force them into the struggle as allies of the working class. But what of the other strata? Their role is crucially important in determining the shape of a national struggle.

It has always been held in the past that the emergence of an African middle class proper was prevented by the denial of land ownership. There have also been some crippling restrictions on business rights in the urban areas where African commerce showed signs of taking off. Notwithstanding these restrictions, however, there has emerged a fairly large sector of salaried, semi–professional and trading people both in the towns and the homelands. There are also a growing number of

113

black civil servants in the homelands, though they are still only appointed to lower grades and act under white supervision.

The question arises whether this sector is in any sense an in-between stratum, having a stake in the system, as collaborators with the ruling class. All the evidence leads against this conclusion. Even civil servants in the corrupt administration in the 'homelands' face two ways. They are dependent on white authority but nevertheless answerable to some degree to the African masses. Outside the reserves Africans are drawn into government administration only at very low levels and their loyalty is minimal.

Even if one were to concede that the semi-professional and trading sectors were not wholly committed to opposing the system at present, it is clear that these groups, which are small in numbers, cannot become a force in their own right. They have power only in combination with the deprived masses.

These factors have led the liberation movement in the past to believe that a neo-colonial solution was not possible and that the call for national liberation would gain the support of Africans of all strata. Recent developments in the Bantustans, where there has been some collusion with the government on the part of 'homeland' leaders, have brought into question the role that these men will play as the struggle unfolds. Whatever these leaders may do, however, there can be little doubt that they cannot satisfy the needs and aspirations of the bulk of the rural population and that opposition to the government will not be blunted. There are even signs that the political jockeying now going on is increasing militancy and political involvement rather than the reverse.

The complexity of the structure of the African people, together with the particular forms that oppression and exploitation take on in South Africa, makes an outright socialist programme unrealistic at this stage. No section of the movement has urged this in the past, and while some groups in exile like PAC and the Communist Party have periodically turned to Marxist phraseology, all have agreed that the primary goal at present is the achievement of national liberation – though it is also held that there will be an ongoing development into socialism thereafter.

Some sympathisers of South African liberation have reservations on the grounds that the movement appears to be subordinating socialist goals to black nationalism. They believe that black nationalism has proved sterile in the rest of Africa and fear that unless socialism is incorporated in the liberation movement's objectives now, the revolution will misfire and bring to power not a people's democratic government oriented to socialism but a black bourgeois-type government which would be no less exploitative than the present white capitalist class.

Socialists in the liberation movement recognise the absolutely vital role of carrying out specifically socialist propaganda both inside the movement and among the

115

masses and of generating the will for a socialist road at all levels. They also believe that the long struggle experience in South Africa, in which the working class has played a major part both in action and in framing ideology, cannot be frustrated by a reformist solution. Furthermore, since there is no prospect of a peaceful solution and armed conflict is only too certain, the forces of liberation must be popular, of a mass character, and revolutionary rather than elitist or reformist in outlook.

The structure of South African economic power is also favourable to an ultimately socialist solution. For instance, we cannot envisage the possibility of the high points of the capitalist structure being entered by any sector of the black people and used for their own enrichment. Furthermore, a large sector of industry is run as state corporations and would be part of the prize of national liberation for the oppressed as a whole.

Given the favourable circumstances there is good reason to predict that a black liberation struggle will produce a progressive government. Support for this view is to be found in the character of the leadership and cadres of the ANC, in the importance given to continuing collaboration with the Communist Party and, above all, in the generally progressive positions taken by the ANC on international questions.

But no matter how auspicious may be the future of socialism, the national aspect of the liberation struggle remains primary, with the African people its determining component.

If African demands are to be in the forefront for political reasons, this is no less important strategically.

The strategic importance of African action is highlighted by the fact that Africans live and work in large numbers in the major urban areas in the country. Not only are Africans the largest population group in almost every urban area but they are the largest group in the industrial labour force as well as being numerically significant in the white residential areas by virtue of domestic employment. In the black housing complexes, the size of the African presence is massive. Despite all the talk of separate development, the permanent African population in a city like Johannesburg is large and well exceeds the total white population. If the 'non-permanent' migratory African population is added, Africans outnumber whites by more than two to one.

In the white farming areas Africans are vastly predominant, with some 3,653,000 as against 600,000 whites. Most physical farming work is done by Africans with whites acting as overseers and managers.

In the Bantustan areas the potential of African power is obvious. While the official leaders spar with government over the degree of autonomy they have, real resistance will grow among the mass of impoverished Africans, which will either force the official leaders into greater militancy or bring them under popular attack. This is what happened in the rural rebellions of the 1950s and in the classic Pondo Revolt of 1960.

If anything, recent government manipulation of the

Bantustan scheme has quickened the pace of political involvement in these areas and mass unrest is very near the surface. Perhaps of decisive importance for the future struggle is the possibility that in the Bantustans there may develop the kind of communal solidarity which enables armed guerrillas to set up bases. Once this happens, the whole character of the confrontation between white rulers and the black mass will be rapidly transformed throughout the country. While it is impossible to predict whether sustained struggle will begin in the countryside and then spread to the towns or vice versa, there can be little doubt about the potential for militant mass action awaiting release in both spheres.

What needs to be done is to harness the overwhelming sense of hostility to the white state and its agencies in the name of non-collaboration and non-cooperation. It seems to me that these concepts have a great deal to offer in the South African situation where one of the first tasks of resistance is to undermine the institutional practices of white rule. The guiding idea is to make it as difficult as possible for the government and authority at all levels to carry out their tasks, and this means rallying the black people in the name of resistance and national liberation. If white rule and white oppression are highlighted sharply in the process, it is history and racism which are at fault.

Will such a policy not block off the possibility of a split in the ruling class?

It must be conceded that it is extremely difficult to carry out a policy that highlights black solidarity and yet maintains an open door to white defection and split. The first condition is necessary to rally the masses, the second to ensure the most favourable conditions for the resolution of the struggle. But if revolution is seen to be a creative act, as Le Duan has urged, then the issue of black solidarity has to be faced squarely.

Non-cooperation can unleash popular feeling, give it scope in practical tasks and open the way for further struggle. It is capable of application in many subtle ways, some of them merely symbolic, yet effective nevertheless. It is a posture that can grow into resistance in many forms and can be combined with the most dramatic methods of struggle, including sabotage and guerrilla warfare.

I have emphasised the need to find forms and concepts of mass struggle because too often, once the decision is taken to embark on armed struggle, the mobilisation of the masses is relegated to second place. This must not be allowed to happen. The South African struggle will be fierce and it will also be protracted. The participation of the masses must be integrated within the total strategic framework in all its many aspects and phases.

It must not be forgotten that the South African ruling class, unlike that in other 'colonial' situations, is indigenous and cannot retreat. It will cling very stubbornly to its power and we must recognise that it controls a strong, modern state machine too powerful for subversion by a small elite corps.

The government has armed forces of great mobility which can be fairly easily concentrated in one spot and overwhelm an armed group without difficulty. The notion of carrying out armed propaganda operations without widespread organised public support is therefore unthinkable. Given the present lack of a friendly border, the one absolutely essential pre-condition for armed activity is a soundly organised structure with real mass support.

The importance of developing the struggle in a popular form is therefore demonstrated on strategic as well as on political grounds.

Fortunately we live in an era when wars of national liberation are no novelty. Vietnam has set a high standard and now there are other wars of the same type close by in Mozambique and Angola. It will surely not be long before South Africa itself catches fire.

Notes

1. *African Communist*, Jan. 1962, No. 8, p. 25.
2. The application of a structural theory of conflict to South Africa has been dealt with by E. Webster, M.Phil. thesis, York University, 1972.
3. Recognition that there is a deep and peculiar significance in the lot of black workers has recently been given by the US Communist Party. They say: 'Black Americans are triply oppressed: because of race; as workers; as a people.' And this leads them to conclude: 'The struggle for Black Liberation in the United States is today the central, most crucial issue before the entire working class and its allies. The call for "Black Liberation" reaffirms the historical goal of full and unconditional economic, political and social equality for Afro-Americans. More, it calls for recognition by white allies that full freedom can be established *only on such terms and in such forms as seem proper to the black people themselves.* The black liberation movement is at the very heart of the struggle against US imperialism, for the freeing of oppressed peoples must be realized to assure the full freedom of all working people.' And again, 'The struggle against racism, then, is a central part of the class struggle and the basic question facing the entire country today.' This recognition by the US Communist Party that blacks are oppressed threefold is timely. If correct there, how much more so in South Africa where black workers are in the majority. In the South African case the national question must hold the centre of the analysis and of the solution: this is the main point in this article.
4. See the article by Joe Matthews, in *Africa South* (1959), p. 15.

5. The number of African workers in industry rose from 156,000 in 1939 to 245,500 in 1945. In Johannesburg the African population increased by 57 per cent between 1936 and 1946. A. Lerumo, *Fifty Fighting Years*, Inkululeko Publications, London, p. 81.
6. *African Claims*, Preface. Mimeo, 1945, publisher not specified.
7. Self-determination for Africans has long been interpreted in the context of a non-racial state. Clause (d) of the 1943 ANC constitution states: 'To strive for the attainment of universal adult suffrage and the creation of a united democratic South Africa.' Mimeo, 16 December 1943.
8. Mofutsanyana was also a member of the Communist Party. Quoted from *Freedom*, Oct. /Nov. 1943, Vol. 3, No. 4.
9. Peter Walshe, *The Rise of African Nationalism in South Africa: The African National Congress 1912–1952*, C. Hurst & Co., London, 1970, pp. 12 and 13.
10. Anthony Sampson, *The Treason Cage: The Opposition on Trial in South Africa*, Heinemann, 1958.
11. Ibid., p. 78.
12. CYL Basic Policy. A statement quoted in Walshe, *Rise of African Nationalism*, p. 357.
13. Walshe, *Rise of African Nationalism*, p. 353.
14. Quoted by Mofutsanyana in *Freedom*, Oct./Nov. 1943.
15. ANC Youth League Constitution, Mimeo, SA Institute of Race Relations, c.1944.
16. Ibid.
17. 1949 Programme of Action. Quoted in Helen Joseph, *If This Be Treason*, André Deutsch, 1963.
18. Ibid.
19. Writing in 1958 Gwendolyn Carter says: 'The dilemma of Non-European leaders in the Union lies precisely in the fact that their aims are not revolution, though European South Africans seldom seem to recognize this fact … In South Africa, in contrast, Non-European political organisations seek changes within the existing system, not its overthrow. They want a share in political power, not to

oust the Europeans.' Gwendolyn M. Carter, *The Politics of Inequality*, Thames and Hudson, London, Third Edition, 1962, p. 378.

20. *Freedom*, Vol. 1, No .8, Special 1949 Conference Issue.
21. *The Guardian*, 12 January 1950.
22. Ibid.
23. See 'Excerpts from Policy and Program' issued by the ANC (External Mission), Dar-es-Salaam, undated.
24. Gene Sharp stresses that non–violent action includes acts of omission and commission and that it is action and not inaction. Adam Roberts (ed.), *Civilian Resistance as a National Defence*, Pelican, 1969, p. 109.
25. *The Guardian*, 22 December 1949.
26. *The Guardian*, 21 January 1950.
27. *The Guardian*, 6 July 1950.
28. *The Guardian*, 27 December 1951.
29. The document sets out the following fundamental principle: 'All people, irrespective of the national groups they may belong to and irrespective of the colour of their skin, are entitled to live a full and free life on the basis of the fullest equality. Full democratic rights with a direct say in the affairs of the government are the inalienable rights of every man – a right which in South Africa must be realised now if the country is to be saved from social chaos and tyranny and from the evils arising out of the existing denial of franchise to vast masses of the population on grounds of race and colour. The struggle which the national organisations of the non–European people are conducting is not directed against any race or national group, but against the unjust laws which keep in perpetual subjection and misery vast sections of the population. It is for the creation of conditions which will restore human dignity, equality and freedom to every South African.' Report of the Joint Planning Council of the African National Congress and the South African Indian Congress, 8 November, 1951. Appendix C, in Leo Kuper, *Passive Resistance in SA*, Jonathan Cape, 1956.
30. *The Guardian*, 20 December 1951.

31. Quoted in Kuper, *Passive Resistance*, p. 233.

32. Explaining the dissolution of the CP in 1950 the official history of the CP says: 'A certain tendency towards legalistic illusions had penetrated the Party and sections of its leadership.' Lerumo, *Fifty Fighting Years*, p. 91.

33. Kuper, *Passive Resistance*, p. 140 and Carter says: 'Even before these measures became law, the resistance campaign was dying down, partly through lack of funds, partly because the stock of volunteers was running low, partly because of the growth of European antagonism, and of tension among the Non-Europeans.' Carter, *Politics of Inequality*, p. 375.

34. Kuper, *Passive Resistance*, p. 42.

35. Leo Kuper, 'Non-Violence Revisited' in *Protest and Power in Black Africa*, *ed.* R.I. Rotberg and Ali A. Mazuri, O.U.P., New York, 1970, p. 793.

36. Kuper said in 1953: 'The defiance acts themselves were so planned, and for the most part so executed, as to give the minimum offence to the sentiments of the whites. The hope for cooperation is expressed in the appeal to Government for the repeal of its own discriminatory laws, in the ready assumption that large sections of the white population are opposed to apartheid, and in the repeated invitations to whites for support in order to prevent the antagonistic separation of the races.' Kuper, *Passive Resistance*, p. 43.

37. Nehru has also commented on the polarisation effect even of non-violent action. He says that previously indifferent people become enthusiasts while opponents become even more hostile. Jawaharlal Nehru, *An Autobiography*, John Lane, The Bodley Head, 1942, p. 545.

38. De Crespigny says that a government must act to assert its authority. 'It is in the process of asserting its authority against political law-breakers that a government may find itself in difficulties. For, in enforcing the law against a large number of resisters, the machinery of law-enforcement is likely to become, so to speak, clogged up with human bodies.' These, says de Crespigny, will consume much judicial time, strain police resources and prisons. The

government may resort to counter measures but these may in turn intensify opposition. Anthony de Crespigny, 'The Nature and Methods of Non–violent Coercion', *Political Studies* (London), Vol. XII, No. 2, June 1964, p. 263.

39. There is an obvious parallel in the case of India. Nehru said in 1936: 'In a political sense the non–violent movement has not succeeded so far, for India is still held in the vice–like grip of Imperialism. In a social sense it has not even envisaged a radical change. And yet anyone with the slightest penetration can see that it has marked a remarkable change in India's millions … It has brought about that quickening process in the masses that precedes revolutionary change.' Nehru, *Autobiography*, p. 538.

40. Mandela warned in an interview (*People's World*, 20 February 1951): 'I hope that Europeans will not form a united front against the Non-Europeans as a result of the Defiance Campaign. To do so would be digging their own grave. The campaign is a non–racial movement with the aim of securing democracy for all. The formation of a European front would turn the whole movement into a racial front with disastrous consequences for all.' The problem was that the united white front was already in existence.

41. Some commentators, e.g. Feit and Walsh, blame the failure on organisational weaknesses in the ANC. This is to beg the question of why it was badly organised if this was the case. The CYL had argued that the prosecution of a militant campaign would build organisation and they were proved right and Dr Xuma wrong.

42. That concentrating on the technique is sterile is evident in Sharp's article in *Peace News*, 25 October 1963. Sharp argues that if an action fails it is not good enough to blame the technique but that the actionists may have failed to apply it efficiently. This is reducing politics to a mechanistic level. If people fail to apply a technique properly, and I would dispute that this was the case in South Africa, then one must surely seek the *political* answer on why they failed to do so. Violence was not finally resorted to as a 'quick answer'. It came very reluctantly, and after an excessive

delay, for the reason that the liberation movement had
not worked out the reasons for earlier frustration or the
character of the political system which made such failure
inevitable as long as one worked within its framework.

43. Liddell Hart has said that non-violent action has had
considerable success but mainly against opponents whose
code of morality was fundamentally similar, and whose
ruthlessness was thereby restrained. Roberts, *Civilian
Resistance*, p. 240.

44. Kuper poses the question: 'What social conditions indicate
the feasibility of fundamental political change by non-
violent means? I shall discuss three such conditions: the
interdependence of the antagonists, the possibility of some
point of reconciliation in the conflict of values and goals,
and the mediating role of a third party.' Kuper, 'Non-
Violence', p. 799.

45. Leo Kuper, 'Some Aspects of Violence and Non-Violent
Political Changes in Plural Societies' in *Pluralism in Africa*,
ed. Leo Kuper and M.G. Smith, University of California
Press, Berkeley and Los Angeles, 1969, p. 160.

46. For a general discussion on 'openness' see T. Ebert in
Roberts, *Civilian Resistance*, p. 305.

47. Luthuli made an interesting statement on this question.
'The emergence of cooperation between people of different
races [in the movement] is one of the most hopeful advances
of the last twelve years, not merely because it increases the
impact of resistance, but because it is the beginning of a
non-racial South Africa ... Tactically, the drawing in of our
horns and the concentration of our forces may have some
advantages, but in the long run it will obstruct the way
to a South Africa which embraces all her citizens.' Albert
Luthuli, *Let My People Go*, Collins, 1962, p. 186.

48. Fatima Meer discusses this in 'African Nationalism: Some
Inhibiting Factors', in H. Adam, *Sociological Perspectives*,
O.U.P., 1971.

49. Ibid.

50. Perhaps they had an instinctive understanding of sociology!
Kuper has suggested that the demand for democracy by

Africans was couched in terms upheld by white society. 'Yet
the realisation of these values throughout the society would
be subversive of the existing social structure, since the
effect would be to liberate the non-whites from domination.'
Leo Kuper, 'The Background to Passive Resistance (South
Africa, 1952)', *British Journal of Sociology*, Vol. IV, No. 3.
Sept. 1953, p.243.

51. In the former category are Gwendolyn Carter in *The
Politics of Inequality*, and Janet Robertson, *Liberalism in
South Africa 1948–1963*, Clarendon Press, Oxford, 1971.
Joe Matthews is quoted as holding the latter position in
Robertson, p. 173.

52. *Africa South*, Oct.–Dec. 1958.

53. For a useful review see Barbara Rogers, *The Bantu
Homelands*, International Defence and Aid Fund, London,
1972.

54. Muriel Horrell, *Action, Reaction and Counter-Action*,
Institute of Race Relations, Johannesburg, 1971, p. 32.

55. See *The Pondo Revolt* by Ben Turok, New Age, Cape
Town, 1961.

56. Ibid., p. 36.

57. However, that the ANC was the first to formulate the
plan for the campaign is conceded by a generally hostile
commentator, Feit, Edward, *Urban Revolt in South Africa
1960–64*, Northwestern University Press, 1971, p. 37.

58. Ibid., p. 40.

59. Horrell, *Action, Reaction*, p. 40.

60. Schelling has hit the nail on the head: 'The case for pure
non-violence is stronger if the object is protest rather than
defence. If one is trying to reach accommodation with a
tyrant, resort to violence may spoil a non-violent bargaining
campaign; but if one is trying to make a tyrant retreat
or withdraw, it is not clear that non-violence by itself is
up to the job, at least within the time span that the word
"defence" suggests.' Roberts, *Civilian Resistance*, p. 354.

61. *Peace News*, 5 July 1963.

62. Feit, *Urban Revolt*, p. 40.

63. *African Communist*, No. 20, 1965, p. 37.

64. Feit, *Urban Revolt*, p. 25.
65. Meer, 'African Nationalism', p. 146.
66. *African Communist*, April 1965, p. 8.
67. Feit, *Urban Revolt*, p. 4.
68. Horrell, *Action, Reaction*, p. 83.
69. *African Communist*, No. 33, 1968, p. 45.
70. *African Communist*, No. 35, 1968, p. 100.
71. *African Communist*, No. 39, 1969, p. 76.
72. *African Communist*, No. 20, 1965, p. 40.
73. Le Duan, *Selected Writings*, Hanoi, 1977.
74. Duplicated copy dated 6 April 1963, issued by National Executive of the ANC.
75. *African Communist*, No. 31, 1967, p. 5; 32, 1968, p. 4; 33, 1968, p. 6.
76. The danger of sending in guerrilla units into territory which had not been prepared politically was well understood. In a statement in August 1965 the Central Committee of the SACP, now in exile, called for greater efforts at home with organisation and propaganda and with mobilising the masses. 'Indeed, it should rather be said that without constant efforts to arouse the resistance and patriotic spirit of the people, activities of a purely military character will become isolated from the people and bound therefore to fail. The real advantage of the liberation forces over all the planes, armoured cars and other superior equipment of the enemy is the support of the masses. This is our decisive weapon, without which we cannot win.' *African Communist*, No. 22, 1965, p. 10.
77. The Johannesburg *Star* reported on 10 May 1963 that a new Defence College had been opened: 'Western powers were more concerned with the conduct of a world war, but South Africa had additional threats to prepare for ... And while other countries worked on the basis of unlimited manpower and weapons deployed in a limited theatre of war, South Africa had to contend with limited manpower and resources in a relatively unlimited theatre of operations.'
78. In a report published in 1968 the SACP stated, 'The

question of armed struggle in South Africa cannot be approached purely as a military question. Particularly in its opening stages, armed conflict cannot take the form of a head-on confrontation with the military and political forces of the South African state. The task of the armed units is basically a political one. Their operations must be designed to help organize and rally the masses, and arouse them to action around their practical problems and grievances.' The document goes on to suggest that guerrilla activities will serve as a powerful stimulant to political organisation and adds, 'But this will not come of its own accord. The duty the political movement owes to the heroic freedom-fighters in the field is to support and to make use of their inspiring struggles by opening new fronts against the oppressor in every possible field of action.' *African Communist*, No. 34, 1968.

79. 'The Strategy and Tactics of the ANC', *Sechaba*, July 1969 (ANC, London).

Index